CULTURES OF THE WORLD
Croatia

Cavendish
Square
New York

Published in 2020 by Cavendish Square Publishing, LLC
243 5th Avenue, Suite 136, New York, NY 10016
Copyright © 2020 by Cavendish Square Publishing, LLC

Third Edition

This publication represents the opinions and views of the author based on his or her personal experience, knowledge, and research. The information in this book serves as a general guide only. The author and publisher have used their best efforts in preparing this book and disclaim liability rising directly or indirectly from the use and application of this book.
All websites were available and accurate when this book was sent to press.

Library of Congress Cataloging-in-Publication Data

Names: Cooper, Robert, 1945 August 2- author | Spilling, Michael, author. |
   Nevins, Debbie, author.
Title: Croatia / Robert Cooper and Michael Spilling ; Debbie Nevins.
Description: Third edition. | New York : Cavendish Square Publishing, 2020.
   | Series: Cultures of the world | Includes bibliographical references
   and index. | Audience: Ages 10 | Audience: Grades 4-6 | Summary:
   "Croatia is a country with a vast history that has survived times of war
   and conflict to now enjoy growth and prosperity. Today, Croatia is a
   place where tourists find and enjoy beautiful havens and stunning
   landscapes. This book offers readers the chance to see what life in
   Croatia is like, including details of its history, government,
   lifestyle, sport, and popular foods. Vivid photographs, detailed
   descriptions of key locations, and compelling sidebars are sure to
   entice and encourage budding explorers"-- Provided by publisher.
Identifiers: LCCN 2019026941 (print) | LCCN 2019026942 (ebook) | ISBN
   9781502650689 (library binding) | ISBN 9781502650696 (ebook)
Subjects: LCSH: Croatia--Juvenile literature.
Classification: LCC DR1510 .C66 2020 (print) | LCC DR1510 (ebook) | DDC
   949.72--dc23
LC record available at https://lccn.loc.gov/2019026941
LC ebook record available at https://lccn.loc.gov/2019026942

Writers, Robert Cooper and Michael Spilling; Debbie Nevins, third edition
Editorial Director, third edition: Katherine Kawa
Editor, third edition: Debbie Nevins
Art Director, third edition: Andrea Davison-Bartolotta
Designer, third edition: Jessica Nevins
Production Manager, third edition: Rachel Rising
Cover Picture Researcher: Jessica Nevins
Picture Researcher, third edition: Jessica Nevins

$ 32.⁵⁰

Printed in the United States of America

CONTENTS

CROATIA TODAY   **5**

1. GEOGRAPHY

Topography • The Adriatic coast • The Dinaric Alps • The Pannonian Plain • Flora and fauna • Climate • Rivers • Cities   **11**

2. HISTORY

From the Illyrians to the Romans • Enter the Croats • Christianity takes root • Between East and West • Seeking unity • Yugoslavia • The Yugoslav Wars • Independence and war • Peace and consequences   **23**

3. GOVERNMENT

The constitution • The executive branch • The legislature • The judiciary • Local government • Foreign relations   **41**

4. ECONOMY

Industry • Agriculture and forestry • Tourism • Energy sources • Working life • Infrastructure   **49**

5. ENVIRONMENT

Air pollution • Water resources • Waste management • Forests and woodlands • Protected areas • Endangered species   **59**

6. CROATIANS

Ethnic groups • The Croatian diaspora • Social hierarchies • Costume   **73**

7. LIFESTYLE

The life cycle • The family • Education • Health • The position of women   **81**

8. RELIGION   Catholics • Protestants • Islam • Orthodoxy • Judaism   **87**

9. LANGUAGE   Historical development • The written language • The spoken language • Greetings • The media   **93**

10. ARTS   Music • The performing arts • Painting • Literature • Film • Folk art • Folk music and dance   **99**

11. LEISURE   Cultural activities • Traditional games • Sports • Sailing and diving • Hunting • Health spas • Nightlife • Shopping   **111**

12. FESTIVALS   Religious holidays • Traditional festivals • Arts and summer fests   **119**

13. FOOD   Foreign influence • Regional specialties • Dessert • Eating out   **125**

MAP OF CROATIA   **133**

ABOUT THE ECONOMY   **135**

ABOUT THE CULTURE   **137**

TIMELINE   **138**

GLOSSARY   **140**

FOR FURTHER INFORMATION   **141**

BIBLIOGRAPHY   **142**

INDEX   **143**

CROATIA TODAY

THROUGHOUT MUCH OF THE TWENTIETH CENTURY, CROATIA WAS part of a larger country called Yugoslavia, located in Central and Southeast Europe. Digging more deeply into history, however, reveals a Croatian statehood in one form or another in this region dating back many centuries. Though the roots of the name—Hrvatska, as the Croatians themselves call it—are uncertain, a "land of the Croats" has existed on and off since 879 CE.

Situated between the Pannonian Plain to the north, the Adriatic Sea to the west, and the mountainous Balkan Peninsula to the south, Croatia is a crescent- or wishbone-shaped country of 4.3 million people. It is home to ancient Greek and Roman ruins, magnificent Gothic and Baroque architecture, spectacular national parks, and nearly 1,200 islands nestled along its extraordinarily beautiful 1,104-mile-long (1,777-kilometer-long) coastline.

Dominated by larger foreign neighbors for much of its history, Croatia emerged from the breakup of the former Yugoslavia in the early 1990s. A bloody and divisive war of independence followed, ending in 1995. The war damaged the nation in many ways that are still being felt, from the disruption and loss of lives to the expenses

A water tower in Vukovar is being built as a symbol of the city's suffering in the Croatian War of Independence.

incurred in rebuilding. Some beautiful towns, such as Dubrovnik and Vukovar, were badly damaged in the war but have now been rebuilt.

Since its rebirth, Croatia has struggled to stabilize itself as a new democracy, but it has largely succeeded, albeit imperfectly. Nevertheless, peace has held, and the country's acceptance into the European Union (EU) in 2013 was widely seen as a sign of progress.

With the threat of wartime violence fading further into the past, Croatia now hopes to entice more visitors. Tourism is its most important industry. The country's magnificent Dalmatian coast has long been a destination for European travelers. The Adriatic waters are clear, with many miles of beaches offering all the usual sea sports and activities. The islands feature charming towns of red-roofed buildings mixed among ancient ruins.

Unlike in many countries, Croatia's capital city, Zagreb, is not its top tourist attraction. That is the medieval city of Dubrovnik, located on the southern tip

of Croatia's coastline. The "Pearl of the Adriatic" includes a fortified, walled "Old Town" section that was named a UNESCO World Heritage site in 1979. Despite that designation as a historical treasure, the city was heavily shelled during a Serb invasion in 1991. Since being repaired according to UNESCO's careful guidelines, the city is once again attracting tourists—so many that it's actually overwhelmed.

In 2018, Dubrovnik officials had to take steps to reduce the hordes of visitors, especially in the Old Town section, in order to protect against the hazards of severe overcrowding. It doesn't help that the wildly popular TV series *Game of Thrones* filmed certain scenes in the city over its eight-season run. Now those sites are attracting fans of the fantasy series in addition to the usual cruise ship crowds.

After Venice, Dubrovnik has become the second most popular cruise destination in the Mediterranean—a blessing that has become more of a curse.

The turquoise waters of the Adriatic contrast with the red roofs and white walls of Old Town Dubrovnik.

Crowds of tourists enjoy a beach in Dubrovnik. Despite overcrowding in this historic city, Croatia is trying to attract more tourists to other areas of the country.

The crowds upset the city's normal way of life, and many locals are leaving to escape the constant carnival atmosphere. Crowds of tourists bring money, but they also bring pollution and detract from the authenticity of the place.

Zagreb lies to the north and far inland, on the upper arm of Croatia's unusual shape. One arm of the country's wishbone shape stretches down the Adriatic coast in the Dalmatia region, while the other, upper arm reaches far inland into the flat plains of Slavonia. Dalmatia and Slavonia are two of the four historical regions that make up the country. Slavonia, a largely agricultural and winemaking region, is a center of folklore and traditional culture.

Zagreb lies in the part of the country called Croatia Proper. It has plenty of attractions of its own. In addition to being the seat of government, it's also a hub for transportation and business and a center of culture, education, and sports. Its annual Christmas market is an enormously popular tourist destination and one that's not dependent on summer vacation weather.

The fourth part of Croatia is Istria. Part of a large peninsula that extends into the Adriatic Sea, it is Croatia's westernmost region. Its close proximity to Slovenia and Italy makes it an ethnically diverse region, with many citizens speaking Italian or Slovenian in addition to Croatian.

One thing all of Croatia's regions have in common is their strong Roman Catholic culture. This, as much as anything, pulls the nation toward Western Europe, an orientation which is now reinforced by its entry into the EU.

This aerial view shows the land formations of Cape Kamenjak in Istria.

However, Croatia's identity is more complicated. For centuries, it has functioned as a geopolitical and cultural borderland between East and West. The historical influences of the ancient Greeks, Romans, Byzantines, Franks, Hungarians, Ottomans, and Venetians have all left their marks. More recently, Croatia's time as a part of the larger, Eastern-leaning, socialist Yugoslavia influenced it in other ways. Yet, through all of these eras, the essential Croatian identity remained intact. Today, Croatians can explore and express that heritage and culture in their own sovereign nation.

GEOGRAPHY

Plitvice Lakes National Park in central Croatia contains sixteen lakes, all connected by waterfalls.

THE EASTERN SHORE OF THE Adriatic Sea is said to be one of the most beautiful in the Mediterranean. With soaring mountains, limestone cliffs, white sand beaches, red-roofed villages, and a multitude of islands, these 1,104 miles (1,777 km) of rugged and picturesque coastline are in Croatia.

Croatia is located in Southeast Europe on the western side of the Balkan region. In all, the country has a total land area of 21,851 square miles (56,594 square kilometers), slightly smaller than the state of West Virginia. However, its shape is nothing like that of West Virginia. It is, rather, a sort of boomerang-shaped country, with one length running down the Adriatic coast and the other extending deep into the mainland of Southeast Europe.

Croatia shares 1,231 miles (1,982 km) of land border with five countries—Slovenia and Hungary in the north, Bosnia and Herzegovina (which is one country) and Serbia in the east, and Montenegro in the south. It also shares sea borders with Slovenia, Montenegro, and Italy.

The republic is made up of three historical regions—Slavonia in the northeast, Istria to the west, and Dalmatia, which lies along the Adriatic coast. Connecting all three of these regions is Central Croatia, or Croatia Proper, home of the capital city, Zagreb.

1

The island of Korčula, just off the Dalmatian coast, is the second most populous of Croatia's Adriatic islands, after Krk. It's also said to be the birthplace of the explorer Marco Polo in 1254, though Venice and Istanbul (then Constantinople) also make that claim.

TOPOGRAPHY

Geographically, Croatia is divided into three parts—the Adriatic coast in the southwest, where mountains slope into the Adriatic Sea and emerge as more than one thousand islands; the Dinaric Mountains, a mountain range that runs parallel to the coast, stretching from northwest to southeast; and, beyond the mountains, the Pannonian Plain.

THE ADRIATIC COAST

The Adriatic coast, which extends from the Gulf of Venice in the north to the Gulf of Kotor in the south, is one of the most irregular coastlines in the world. Croatia's Adriatic coastline is bordered by more than 1,185 islands

This map of Croatia shows some of its most important cities.

(the exact number varies according to definition)—the largest archipelago in the Mediterranean Sea.

Only forty-seven islands are inhabited year-round, although as many as sixty-six have been inhabited in the past. The largest are Cres, Krk, Pag, Rab, and Lošinj along the northern coast; Dugi Otok, Kornat, Ugljan, and Pasman in the center; and Brač, Hvar, Korčula, Pelješac, and Mljet in the south. About one hundred islands are temporarily occupied during the tourist or fishing seasons. Each of the islands of Krk, Korčula, Brač, and Hvar has a population of between ten thousand and twenty thousand people.

THE DINARIC ALPS

Rising steeply from the turquoise sea and yellow beaches, the Dinaric Alps follow the coastal northwest-southeast finger of Croatia and continue into

Since 1975, the United Nations Educational, Scientific and Cultural Organization (UNESCO) has maintained a list of international landmarks or regions considered to be of "outstanding universal value" to the people of the world. Such sites embody the common natural and cultural heritage of humanity and therefore deserve particular protection. The organization works with the host country to establish plans for managing and conserving its sites. UNESCO also reports on sites which are in imminent or potential danger of destruction and can offer emergency funds to try to save the property.

The organization is continually assessing new sites for inclusion on the World Heritage list. In order to be selected, a site must meet at least one of ten criteria. These required elements include cultural value—that is, artistic, religious, or historical significance—and natural value, including exceptional beauty, unusual natural phenomena, and scientific importance.

As of 2019, there are 1,092 sites listed, including 845 cultural, 209 natural, and 38 mixed properties in 167 nations. Of those, 54 are listed as "in danger." In Croatia, eight cultural sites and one natural site are on the main list, and none are in danger. Croatia's World Heritage sites include: the historical complex of Split and the ruins of Diocletian's Palace, the old city of Dubrovnik, the historic city of Trogir (shown below), the Cathedral of St. James in Šibenik, and four other cultural sites. Its natural site is Plitvice Lakes National Park. Croatia is also one of twelve countries that share a transboundary listing, the ancient, primeval beech forests of Europe.

The spectacular scenery of Plitvice Lakes National Park attracts one million visitors each year.

neighboring Bosnia and Herzegovina, where some of the highest peaks are found. In Croatia, the mountains are usually several hundred feet below the highest peak, Mount Dinara, which stands 6,006 feet (1,830 meters) above sea level. This region has a unique geological feature—a terrace made of karst, a soft limestone that is easily eroded into unusual shapes. Also found in the mountains are the Plitvička Jezera, or Plitvice Lakes. These sixteen lakes, which only cover an area of 490 acres (198 hectares), are thought to have been formed four thousand years ago. They are connected by ninety-two waterfalls. The site was placed on the UNESCO World Heritage List of natural places in 1979.

THE MYTH OF MLJET

The southernmost of the Adriatic islands off the Dalmatian coast is Mljet (m'LET). It's a long, thin island about 23 miles (37 km) long by about 2 miles (3.2 km) wide. Its jagged coast is dotted with coves, cliffs, inlets, and bays. The island has a reputation as the most beautiful, lush, and green of Croatia's islands, and about one-third of it is protected as a national park.

Mljet also has another reputation, based in legend. A rocky cave on the island's rugged southern shore is called Odysseus Cave—named for the mythological Greek hero. In Homer's ancient Greek classic the Odyssey, *the hero Odysseus is shipwrecked on his long journey home to Ithaca from the ten-year Trojan War. He washes ashore*

into a cave on Ogygia, an island ruled by the beautiful nymph Calypso. The goddess holds him captive for seven years, hoping to make him her immortal husband. To keep him from escaping, she beguiles him with her singing.

According to local legend, Mljet is the enchanted Ogygia, and the sea cave is the spot where Odysseus swam to land. It seems to be irrelevant that Mljet is not on the way from ancient Troy (thought to have been in today's Turkey) to the Greek island of Ithaca—after all, Odysseus was really lost. It also seems to be irrelevant that Gozo, an island of Malta, farther west in the Mediterranean Sea, also claims to have been Ogygia and boasts its own Odysseus Cave. It also doesn't matter that the Odysseus story is fiction! What does matter is that Mljet and its cave are special places in themselves and great tourist attractions.

A tractor sits in a field in Slavonia, in the Pannonian Plain region of Croatia.

THE PANNONIAN PLAIN

Mountains rise steeply from the coast, then slope away in the north of Croatia to the Pannonian Plain. It was so named because in prehistory, the area formed the inland Pannonian Sea. Today, the shallow Lake Balaton in Hungary is the last remnant of this ancient sea.

The flat plains, which are located between the Sava and Drava Rivers, are the most fertile part of the country due to the alluvial soil from the two rivers. The area is referred to as the "Croatian granary" and produces high yields of wheat, corn, sugar beets, sunflowers, alfalfa, and clover. There is a saying that the farmers and culture of the region are as rich as the soil. The region also has oil and gas deposits.

FLORA AND FAUNA

Croatia's coastal and lower altitude mountain regions are part of a large ecoregion of Europe called the Illyrian deciduous forests. This area is rich in plant and animal species, partly because of the comparatively low population density. Bears, wolves, long-eared owls, chamois, lynx, deer, and marsh birds are plentiful. Many areas have been designated national parks or special reserves, where hunting and collecting are forbidden. Nevertheless, illegal logging, illegal hunting, and uncontrolled plant harvesting have destroyed extensive forest areas that had been relatively intact until recently.

The mountains, hillsides, and gorges provide a large quantity of wood from beech, oak, ash, cherry, and black pine trees. This is used by the domestic furniture industry and exported in the form of furniture and parquet flooring to the rest of Europe and the United States. The most abundant plant life is in the mountains of the Velebit Nature Park, including some seventy-five plants native to the region. In contrast, a different type of vegetation can be found along the Adriatic coast, where cypresses, laurels, oleanders, aloes, and olive and fig trees thrive. More than 360 species of fish can be found in Croatia's clear waters. There are also sponges and corals.

The long-eared owl (*asio otus*), is a common species in Croatia.

CLIMATE

The three geographic regions of Croatia have distinct climates. The Adriatic coast enjoys long, warm summers, when high temperatures are cooled by sea breezes to an average 77 degrees Fahrenheit (25 degrees Celsius), and short, mild winters, when the heat stored in the sea during the summer warms the land. January temperatures range from 41°F (5°C) to 50°F (10°C).

The Pannonian region has a continental climate of cold winters and hot summers. The Dinaric Alps experience an Alpine climate of long, cold winters and short summers; even on the coldest day, when snow covers the land, the sun often shines.

There are four kinds of wind phenomena in Croatia. The strongest is the *bora*, a northeasterly wind that can reach speeds of up to 124 miles (200 km) per hour, causing damage on land and disruption in sea transportation. The gentle *yugo* blows from the south and is welcomed for the rain it brings to the plains. The *mistral* is a mild summer breeze that blows from the sea to the land and cools the hotter inland days. The *zgorac* blows from the land toward the sea.

RIVERS

The significant rivers in Croatia are the Sava, Drava, and Neretva. The Sava runs for three-quarters of its 584-mile (940 km) length inside Croatia's boundaries. The capital city of Zagreb is built on the banks of the Sava. The Drava makes a third of its 465-mile (749 km) journey through Croatia. The Neretva, although a more modest 143 miles (230 km) long, provides the largest flow of water from Croatia into the Adriatic Sea. Only a third of Croatia's rivers flow into the Adriatic; most drain to the east into the Black Sea.

A green railway bridge crosses the Sava River in Zagreb.

Of the three major rivers, only the Sava is navigable throughout its course. Some rivers are only partly navigable because of high waterfalls. In the nineteenth and early twentieth centuries, when rivers were used to transport goods and deploy armed forces, these waterfalls were considered a nuisance. Today, the rivers and waterfalls are a welcome source of hydroelectric energy.

CITIES

Croatia has been an urban country for many centuries, with almost 60 percent of the population living in towns and cities. Many of the towns date back to medieval times. Towns are more numerous in Croatia than in any other similarly sized area in Southeast Europe. Zagreb, the capital, has a population of about 700,000. Smaller cities include Split (with a population of 176,000), Zadar (71,300), and Dubrovnik (28,400).

Split lies on the Adriatic coast, in the Dalmatia region, backed by the Mosor Mountains.

CITIES UNDER FIRE

Historic Croatian cities such as Dubrovnik, Vukovar, and Osijek were badly damaged during the War of Independence of 1991–1995. These were the urban centers nearest to neighboring Serbia. Dubrovnik was hit by some two thousand shells in 1991 and 1992. Two-thirds of the 824 Old Town buildings were damaged. The cost of replacing the unique terra-cotta roofs and repairing the fine white limestone walls was estimated at more than $10 million. Because of the importance of Dubrovnik to world heritage and Croatian tourism, restoration work was rapid, and by 2005, most of the city had been repaired.

Baroque-style Vukovar (a damaged building there is shown below), which links Croatia and Serbia with its famous bridge across the Danube River, was not so lucky. A locally organized militia defended the town from a Serb attack for almost three months. More than two thousand defenders and civilians were killed during the siege, with a further twenty thousand forced to flee. The city has been slowly reconstructed since the end of the war, and refugees have returned to the town to rebuild their lives and homes. On November 18, 2006, approximately twenty-five thousand people from all over Croatia gathered in Vukovar on the fifteenth anniversary of the fall of the city to commemorate those who died during the war.

VUKOVAR

Croatia's Roman ruins include an amphitheater in Pula (one of the world's best preserved). In Split, the monumental palace of Emperor Diocletian, dating from the third century CE, is recognized as the finest surviving example of classical defensive architecture in Europe. It is also a UNESCO World Heritage site. In Poreč, the mosaics of the Euphrasius Basilica are excellent examples of Byzantine art from the sixth century CE. The architectural style of Zadar and Ston is Gothic. The Renaissance shaped the character of Pag, Šibenik, Hvar, Korčula, and Dubrovnik, while the Baroque period left its mark on Varaždin and Vukovar.

Most of Croatia's cities have survived invasion and centuries of warfare. Their historic buildings have been modernized to function in contemporary urban centers. The sixteenth-century Sponza Palace in Dubrovnik, which was a customs house, is now home to the State Archives.

INTERNET LINKS

https://www.find-croatia.com/islands-croatia
A map, information, and photos of Croatia's many islands, with links to each, are featured on this travel site.

https://www.thedubrovniktimes.com/information/item/ 1181-mljet-discover-myths-and-secrets-of-the-odysseus-cave
This article is about the Odysseus Cave of Mljet.

https://whc.unesco.org/en/statesparties/hr
The World Heritage List for Croatia has links to each of the cultural, natural, and tentative sites.

https://www.worldatlas.com/webimage/countrys/europe/ croatia/hrland.htm
This site provides a quick overview of Croatia's geography, with maps.

HISTORY

Sculptures at the Neanderthal Museum in Krapina, Croatia, represent some of the region's earliest inhabitants.

2

Croatia's history is long and complicated. It's a story of constantly shifting power dominance, allegiances, and national identities. Throughout it all, the region has stood on the nexus of East and West, a borderland between Western Europe, the Mediterranean, and the Eastern European world.

CROATIA'S HISTORY BEGINS AT THE dawn of humanity. Evidence of early hominids in Croatia goes back some 125,000 years to the Paleolithic period, or Early Stone Age. Bones and craniums of *Homo sapiens neanderthalensis*, or Neanderthals, were found in the caves of Krapina in northern Croatia by the paleontologist Dragutin Gorjanović between 1899 and 1906. In 2010, the Krapina Neanderthal Museum opened near the site. The new, state-of-the-art museum features interactive exhibits; collections of geological, paleontological, and experimental archaeological interest; and life-size sculptures of Neanderthals.

As millennia passed, humans left their caves and settled in agricultural and fishing communities. Extensive excavations at Vučedol, near the eastern Croatian city of Vukovar, revealed artifacts and skeletal remains of what is called the Vučedol culture. Ceramic and copper objects provide insight into the lives of the ancient peoples who inhabited the region from the late Stone Age to the Bronze Age (3000 BCE—2000 BCE). The

Vučedol Culture Museum, which opened in 2013, is a national museum on the banks of the Danube River not far from the archaeological site.

FROM THE ILLYRIANS TO THE ROMANS

Around 1000 BCE, the Illyrians, an Indo-European people, migrated from the east and settled in what is now Croatia. The Illyrians had a warlike reputation. Over a long period of time, they successfully resisted Greek encroachments from Macedonia and from the Adriatic coast and islands.

In the second century BCE, the Romans invaded the Balkan region and eventually took control of the entire area. What is now Croatia became the Roman provinces of Dalmatia and Pannonia. The Romans brought peace to the Balkan region, as they did to most of Europe. By 117 CE, the Roman Empire had reached its greatest extent.

In 395 CE, the Roman Empire divided in two. The Danube River, on Croatia's eastern border, marked the boundary between the Western Roman Empire

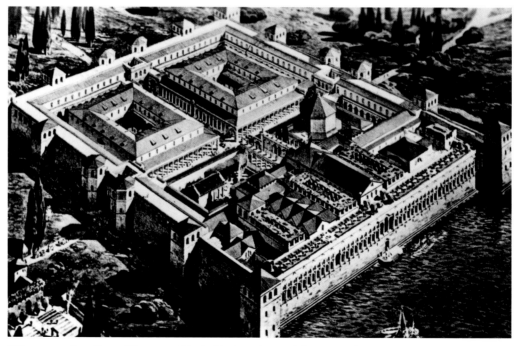

This reconstruction of Emperor Diocletian's palace at Spalatum (modern-day Split), on the coast of Dalmatia, shows what it looked like around 310 CE.

DIOCLETIAN

Born in Dalmatia in 245 CE, a man of lowly origins named Diocles rose to become an emperor of the Roman Empire. In 284, this highly ranked member of the Illyrian army

became Emperor Diocletian. At this time, the empire was in decline, suffering from decades of poor leadership.

To help stabilize the immense empire, he established a system of government called the tetrarchy, or "rule by four." He began by naming his son-in-law Maximian as co-ruler, in charge of the western half of the realm, while Diocletian himself focused on the east, which included his home territory of Dalmatia. Eventually he added two more co-rulers in subordinate positions. Each of the four administered his own territory and had his own capital. For Diocletian, that was Nicomedia, an ancient Greek city (modern Izmit) in what is now Turkey.

One of Diocletian's greatest problems during his reign was the growing popularity of Christianity. He himself would have no part of this new, upstart religion and considered it a threat to his authority, so he sought to stamp it out. In the year 303, he and his three co-rulers issued a series of edicts that became known as the Great Persecution. Christians were deprived of their rights and ousted from the military, and some were imprisoned, enslaved, or tortured and executed. Churches were razed and scriptures burned.

In 305, Diocletian abdicated his throne because of illness and retired to his palace in Spalatum (modern-day Split in Croatia). He remained there until his death in 311. Two years after his death, the Edict of Milan outlawed the persecution of Christians throughout both halves of the empire under the first Christian emperor, Constantine. Today, the ruins of Diocletian's palace and the historic center of Split are a UNESCO World Heritage site.

At first, Diocletian's unique method of shared rule strengthened the empire, but it didn't last long. Instead of peace, his fervor for exterminating Christians brought renewed instability to the realm. Warring among successors eventually brought the tetrarchy to an end. However, the concept of splitting the empire would regain favor later in the fourth century. In 395, the Roman Empire was divided in half for a final time.

and the Eastern Roman, or Byzantine, Empire. Croatia was absorbed into the Western Roman Empire but was on the empire's easternmost edge, its most vulnerable area. The boundaries shifted back and forth over the centuries, however, and at times this region was firmly within the Byzantine realm.

The Byzantine Empire differed from the Roman Empire in that it was centered in Constantinople (rather than Rome), and it was more oriented toward Greek culture—in fact Heraclius, who reigned from 610 to 641, adopted Greek, as opposed to Latin, as Byzantium's official language. After the entire empire adopted Christianity, the Eastern realm followed Eastern Orthodox Christianity while the West followed Roman Catholicism.

ENTER THE CROATS

At this time, Croats, Serbs, and other Slavic tribes were living in a vast swampy terrain north and east of present-day Hungary, possibly in what is now Ukraine. There, they engaged in intermittent conflict with the Avars, who occupied much of the Hungarian plains. The Avars had ambitions of expanding their own fledgling empire at the expense of a weakened Roman Empire and were at this time launching regular attacks into Byzantium.

Emperor Heraclius offered the Croats land on the eastern shore of the Adriatic Sea if they would liberate that and other areas from the Avars, who were a constant threat to the empire. The Croats were so successful that the Avars disappeared from historical record. By the beginning of the seventh century, the Croats had settled throughout most of present-day Croatia and much of present-day Bosnia and Herzegovina and Serbia.

CHRISTIANITY TAKES ROOT

Not much is known about exactly how Christianity came to Croatia. Its influence began to be felt in the fourth and fifth centuries. Churches and shrines were built in Salona, the ancient capital of Dalmatia, at the same time that Emperor Diocletian was living out his final years nearby in Split.

Meanwhile, the Western Roman Empire weakened considerably and ended in 476 CE. Eventually, Western Europe united again under the Frankish kings

(the Carolingians) and converted to Christianity. In 800 CE, the Carolingian emperor Charles the Great (Charlemagne) conquered Dalmatia and urged the Croat rulers to convert to Christianity with a series of mass baptisms.

Under Charlemagne, the Croatia region was organized into two adjoining principalities governed by local princes—the Principality of Dalmatian Croatia in the coastal, mountainous area of southern Croatia, and the Principality of Pannonian Croatia in the lowlands of northern Croatia. That these principalities were roughly the same regions as the old Roman provinces of the same names demonstrates a continuity of place and identity over many centuries, toward the development of a Croatian nationality.

After Charles's death in 814, the Byzantine Empire controlled most of Dalmatia, while the Croats in Pannonia remained under Frankish rule. However,

Ruins of the early Christian basilica of ancient Salona on the Dalmatian coast date to about the fourth century CE.

The Republic of Ragusa was a small, independent maritime republic centered in the city of Dubrovnik on the southernmost part of the Dalmatian coast. It existed from 1358 to 1808, reaching its commercial peak in the fifteenth and the sixteenth centuries, when it was under the protection of the Ottoman Empire. The city was taken by Napoleon Bonaparte's French Empire in 1806. In a region where commercial interests were often paramount, the city had a motto: Non bene pro toto libertas venditur auro *(Latin for "Liberty is better than gold"). Today, it's a part of Croatia.*

The fortress walls of the old part of Dubrovnik date from its time as the Republic of Ragusa.

in 925, a reunited Pannonia and Dalmatia became an independent Croatian kingdom under Duke Tomislav (reigned 910—928). He successfully beat back Magyar (Hungarian) attacks in the north and joined the Serbs to stand against the invading Bulgarians. Tomislav was recognized as king of Croatia by Pope John X, who sent the crown to Tomislav with the message: "To my dear son Tomislav, King of the Croats."

BETWEEN EAST AND WEST

King Stephen II of Croatia died in 1091, leaving no heir. In 1102, Croatia came under the control of neighboring Hungary, although the country maintained self-government. For the next four centuries, Croatia was ruled by local rulers appointed by the Hungarian kings.

In 1205, Venice, a neighboring maritime and trading power, invaded and took control of much of the Istrian and Dalmatian coast. For several centuries, wealthy Venice essentially siphoned off Croatian resources and impoverished the region.

Meanwhile, Ottoman Turkey ruled those parts of Croatia not seized by Venice. In 1526, after the death of King Ludovik II of Hungary, the Habsburgs of Austria claimed the Hungarian throne. The Croatian Sabor (SAH-bor), or parliament, named Archduke Ferdinand I of Austria the king of Croatia. In return for accepting the throne of Croatia, Ferdinand vowed to help it resist an Ottoman invasion. At the end of the seventeenth century, Turkey finally renounced all claims to Croatia.

For centuries, Croatia was pulled back and forth between various powers. Sometimes it existed as a unified region, and other times it was a patchwork of places. Austrian control was briefly interrupted in 1805, when Napoleon Bonaparte beat the Austrian and Prussian forces at Austerlitz and took the Dalmatian coast as one of his prizes. France immediately instituted some improvements in the region, such as a tree-planting campaign to reforest hills that had been stripped by the Venetians in harvesting wood for their ships. France also began efforts to educate the mostly illiterate populace, built roads and hospitals, and undertook other ambitious projects. However, Napoleon's reign did not last long.

The fall of the Napoleonic Empire in 1815 led to the Congress of Vienna, which recognized Austria's claim to Dalmatia, while placing the rest of Croatia under the jurisdiction of Hungary. Austria gave Dalmatia back to its former

This historic marker in Zagreb reads, "Border of the Illyrian Provinces at the time of Napoleon, 1800–1813."

master, Venice, and Hungary immediately sought to impose the Hungarian language and culture throughout its portion of Croatia.

SEEKING UNITY

In 1867, the two powerful countries of Austria and Hungary joined forces to form the Austro-Hungarian Empire. This dual monarchy was not a merger so much as a partnership of two equals. The Kingdom of Croatia—which did not include the Dalmatia or Slavonia regions at the time—was part of the Hungarian-ruled region of the empire.

Ethnic South Slavs were spread among several states under Austro-Hungarian rule. Rising national sentiments spurred a national, political, and cultural campaign led by a nationalist group called the Illyrian Movement. It sought to unite all Slavic peoples within the empire. This proposed nation came to be called Yugoslavia. Other Balkan peoples, especially the Serbs and the

This view of Pula in 1880, at the time of the Austro-Hungarian Empire, shows the Roman amphitheater.

Slovenes, developed similar nationalist yearnings. Some of them eventually merged their goals with the Yugoslavists.

As the nationalist movement grew, Hungary tried to defuse the situation. In 1867, the Croats were given their own parliament and the right to use the Croatian language, but Croatia was still subordinate to Hungary. Although most Croatian opposition remained nonviolent, an armed rebellion broke out in 1871. Even though the uprising failed, it gave the Habsburgs the excuse to expand their control over the whole of Bosnia and Herzegovina. For the remainder of the nineteenth century, the Croatian parliament was dominated by pro-Hungarian and pro-Austrian groups, until a Croat-Serb coalition won parliamentary elections in 1906.

Then, on June 28, 1914, a nineteen-year-old Serb Yugoslavist named Gavrilo Princip shot and killed Archduke Franz Ferdinand and his wife when they were visiting the Bosnian city of Sarajevo. The archduke was heir to the throne of the Austro-Hungarian Empire. The assassination sparked an inferno that quickly raced across Europe and well beyond—World War I. At the time, not realizing there would be a World War II, the world generally referred to the war as the Great War.

YUGOSLAVIA

The end of World War I brought great changes to the Balkan region. The Austro-Hungarian Empire was defeated and broken up into many separate countries. On December 1, 1918, as part of the postwar settlement, the Kingdom of Serbs, Croats, and Slovenes was formed, though the world almost immediately started calling it Yugoslavia. It was headed by the prince regent (later king) Alexander of the Serbian ruling dynasty.

Soon, long-simmering differences between Croats and Serbs erupted into hostilities in the 1920s. Most famously, political disagreements between Croats and Serbs came to a head in 1928 at the June 20 meeting of the Yugoslavian parliament. There, after a good deal of ranting by both sides, a Serbian member of parliament took out a gun and shot five members of the Croatian Peasant Party, killing three of them. At the news of the shootings, demonstrations erupted in Zagreb. Popular support for a unified Kingdom of Serbs, Croats, and

This photo from 1939 shows a Yugoslavian infantry regiment conducting maneuvers in Belgrade.

Slovenes faded fast. To suppress the violence, King Alexander I imposed direct rule in 1929 and renamed the country the Kingdom of Yugoslavia. His move was opposed by a group of young Croats and Macedonians, who assassinated him in 1934.

As World War II broke out in 1939, Yugoslavia was barely holding itself together. In April 1941, the weak Yugoslav army was easily defeated by German and Italian troops after just a few weeks. The Independent State of Croatia was proclaimed that month under a German puppet administration called the Ustaše (OOS-tah-she), or Croatian Revolutionary Movement. These fascist, ultranationalist rulers set up a brutal campaign to cleanse Croatia of Serbs, Roma, and Jews. Not all Croats supported the Ustaše. Yugoslavs were fighting amongst themselves as much as they were fighting against their occupiers, but many joined with Serb partisan groups and fought a vicious war of resistance under Josip Broz Tito (1892—1980) against the German occupation.

TITO

Born Josip Broz in Kumrovec, northwest of Zagreb, in 1892, the son of a Croat father and a Slovene mother, the man now known as Tito was drafted into the Austro-Hungarian army during World War I and taken prisoner by the Russians. He escaped and joined the communist Red Army in 1917, fighting to help establish the Soviet Union. He returned to Croatia in 1920 and, as secretary of the outlawed Communist Party, worked for two decades to increase party membership.

As a result of his communist activities, he was arrested in 1928 and imprisoned for five years. After his release in 1934, he adopted the pseudonym, Tito, after the eighteenth-century Croatian writer Tito Brezovački. When the Germans invaded Yugoslavia in 1941, Tito led a national resistance movement. His campaign of resistance was supported militarily by the Allies.

In 1945, Tito became the first premier of postwar Yugoslavia. He clashed with Soviet leader Joseph Stalin and in 1948 was dismissed from the Cominform, which was an organization set up to share information among European communist parties. For the rest of his life and rule, Tito maintained a neutral position between East and West, holding together the various ethnic groups of Yugoslavia in what has been called a "balance of powers federation."

Tito's autocratic style united Serbs, Croatians, ethnic Albanians, Slovenes, and Macedonians for thirty-five years. Under his astute leadership, Croatia prospered, building huge tourist and shipbuilding industries, as well as a small petrochemical empire. As a communist nation, Yugoslavia was far more open than its communist Eastern European neighbors. In fact, Yugoslavs were free to leave the country at any time—an unheard of liberty in other communist countries—for work or vacation.

When Tito died in May 1980, he was genuinely mourned throughout Yugoslavia. However, no one, it seemed, was able to step into his shoes in terms of keeping the cap on the country's simmering ethnic differences. For ten years after his death, the country was beset by economic problems, ethnic violence, and rival nationalist ideals that eventually led to the destruction of Tito's Yugoslavia.

In Zagreb, Yugoslavia, thousands of people rally to celebrate victory over Nazi Germany and the end of World War II.

With the Allied victory in 1945, the dream of a united Yugoslavia again became a reality, this time under the control of antifascist, communist forces led by Tito. The new country, the Socialist Republic of Yugoslavia, was made up of six republics with separate ethnic identities: Serbia, Slovenia, Croatia, Bosnia and Herzegovina, Montenegro, and Macedonia. Until his death in 1980, Tito controlled Yugoslavia and steered the ruling Yugoslav Communist Party along a neutral path between the neighboring communist Soviet bloc and the Western North Atlantic Treaty Organization (NATO) alliance.

For the next few decades, Serbs and Croatians appeared to have buried their differences. In 1971, however, resentment at the redistribution of Croatia's wealth to the poorer republics in the federation led to a "Croatian Spring" when reformers called for greater economic autonomy. Critics were jailed or removed from positions of influence. In 1974, when the threat from Croatian separatists had passed, the republics were given more autonomy. The stage was thus set for the conflict between the republics that followed the disintegration of communism throughout Eastern Europe in the late 1980s. These national differences, and the collapse of the communist system, led to the breakup of the Socialist Republic of Yugoslavia.

THE YUGOSLAV WARS

As the Soviet Union broke apart in 1990 and 1991, communism likewise fell apart in Eastern Europe. The six republics and two autonomous provinces that made up the Yugoslav federation began to reassert their separate identities. The resulting breakup of Yugoslavia did not go well.

Almost immediately, a series of separate but related wars and conflicts broke out across the region. These wars took place over a ten-year period, from 1991 to 2001, though not every conflict lasted the full ten years. They have come to be called the Yugoslav Wars, but each separate conflict had its own identity. Among them was the Croatian War of Independence, which lasted from 1991 to 1995.

INDEPENDENCE AND WAR

In May 1990, the Croatian Democratic Union (known by the acronym HDZ), headed by Franjo Tudjman, won the Croatian elections. In a referendum a year later, 93 percent of the population of Croatia voted in favor of independence. Following this clear mandate, Croatia declared independence on June 25, 1991.

Meanwhile, a separate country made up of Serbia and Montenegro proclaimed itself the Federal Republic of Yugoslavia, under the rule of strongman Slobodan Milošević. This country tried to inherit the mantle of the former

Yugoslavia, but the other constituent parts of the old alliance objected, and in general, the international community didn't recognize it as such.

In Croatia, Serbian citizens objected to independence. The new Croatian constitution's failure to guarantee minority rights, along with a purge of Serbs from public service, stimulated Croatia's ethnic Serb community of six hundred thousand to rebel. They declared nearly one third of Croatia's territory to be an independent Serb state, the Republic of Serbian Krajina. Violence between Croats and Serbs ensued. The European Union advised Croatia to freeze its declaration of independence for three months to avoid further bloodshed, but the fighting still intensified and spread. Local skirmishes erupted into what is now called the Croatian War of Independence.

Milošević's Yugoslavia backed the Croatian Serbs in their revolt. Serbs throughout the region envisioned a common state with Serbia, incorporating Serb-dominated lands in Croatia and Bosnia. The Serbs expelled Croats and other non-Serbs from their territory in a brutal campaign of "ethnic cleansing." Serb separatists systematically attacked other ethnic groups, subjecting civilians to many atrocities, including torture, murder, and imprisonment in concentration camps.

Serb forces shelled and heavily damaged the ancient city of Dubrovnik, a UNESCO World Heritage site. In the Croatian city of Vukovar, on the far eastern border with Serbia, some two thousand volunteer Croats held out for eighty-seven days against thirty-six thousand Serb troops. The city eventually fell to the invaders. It endured such heavy damage and loss of life that it was called the worst seen in Europe since World War II.

On October 7, 1991, the presidential palace in Zagreb was hit by rockets in a Serb attempt to kill President Tudjman. The following day, October 8, 1991, when the moratorium on independence ended, Croatia declared itself a republic. Croatia's independence was recognized by some one hundred countries, and the new republic was admitted to the United Nations (UN) in 1992. The UN set up four protected areas in Croatia, sending fourteen thousand UN peacekeeping troops to prevent violence between Croats and Serbs.

Amid the violence, many Croatian Serbs fled to Serbia. Likewise, Croatians from neighboring republics settled in Croatia. During 1992 and 1993, an estimated 225,000 Croat refugees fled to Croatia from Bosnia and Herzegovina and Serbia. Most sources agree that up to 20,000 Croatians (both Croats and Serbs) died during the war years of 1991 to 1995.

Negotiated cease-fires brought most fighting in Croatia to a halt by 1994, but war continued to rage in Bosnia, where Croatia was involved in supporting the Bosnian Croats. In November 1995, the Dayton Peace Accords, held in Dayton, Ohio, under the US leadership of President Bill Clinton, ended the war in Bosnia, and by extension, the rest of the Balkans. It was signed by the presidents of Croatia, Bosnia, and Serbia and implemented with the help of NATO troops, including the United States. The accords confirmed Croatian control within the current boundaries of the country.

Leaders of six other nations, including President Bill Clinton (*back row, second from the left*), look on as the presidents of Serbia, Croatia, and Bosnia sign the Dayton Peace Accords.

PEACE AND CONSEQUENCES

As Croatia emerged from years of war, things settled down, and the country worked toward stability. In the 1997 elections, Tudjman and the Croatian Democratic Union were returned to power. Tudjman died in 1999, and in the 2000 parliamentary elections, the nationalist HDZ government was replaced by a center-left coalition, with Ivica Račan as prime minister. At the same time, presidential elections were held, which were won by a moderate, Stjepan Mesić.

In 2003, new parliamentary elections were held, and a reformed but still right-wing HDZ Party won under the leadership of Ivo Sanader, who became the new prime minister. That year, Croatia formally applied for membership in the European Union (EU). The EU delayed approval, expressing concern over corruption in the government.

The North Atlantic Treaty Organization (NATO) is a mutual defense alliance of twenty-nine countries from North America and Europe.

INTERNATIONAL JUSTICE

In 1999, Croatia took its case against Serbia to the International Court of Justice (ICJ) in The Hague, Netherlands. The ICJ, also called the World Court, is the judicial body of the UN. It created the International Criminal Tribunal for the Former Yugoslavia specifically to try criminal cases related to the violence of the 1990s.

Croatia charged Serbia with committing genocide during its "ethnic cleansing" campaign during the War of Croatian Independence, when Serbs took control of one-third of Croatia's territory. Genocide is the deliberate attempt to destroy a large group of people based on their nationality, ethnicity, race, or religion. It is considered a war crime. Croatia's suit against Serbia said more than twelve thousand Croatian civilians were killed during shelling campaigns, thousands were incarcerated in camps, and up to one hundred thousand people fled their homes.

In 2010, with the lawsuit still undecided, Serbia countersued Croatia. Serbia said more than two hundred thousand ethnic Serbs had been forced to flee their homes when Croatia launched a military campaign in 1995 to retake its territory.

In 2015, the court ruled that neither nation was guilty of genocide. However, in other, related cases, the tribunal indicted 161 individuals on various war crimes, including individual counts of genocide. Of those, there were 94 Serbs and 29 Croats, with the remaining few being people from other Balkan regions. Those found guilty included 62 Serbs, 18 Croats, and several others. They ranged from common soldiers to generals and police commanders, right up to prime ministers.

Most famously, perhaps, the president of Serbia and the former Federal Republic of Yugoslavia, Slobodan Milošević, faced sixty-six counts of crimes against humanity, genocide, and war crimes committed during the Yugoslav Wars. He pleaded not guilty to all of them. He died in 2006 in The Hague, while still in custody, before a verdict was reached.

Slobodan Milošević

Sanader resigned in 2009 and was tried on two separate corruption charges in 2011, including taking millions of euros in bribes during the war years, when he was deputy foreign minister. He fled the country but was apprehended and returned. Some of the many legal cases against him are still progressing as of 2019.

In 2009, Croatia joined NATO, and in 2013, it was approved for membership in the EU. In 2016, HDZ leader Andrej Plenković took office as prime minister and established a pro-Europe, moderate-conservative coalition government. He had previously served as the deputy chief of Croatia's mission to the EU.

The European Union (EU) is a political and economic organization of twenty-eight European member nations as of 2019.

INTERNET LINKS

https://www.ancient.eu/Diocletian
The life and times of Diocletian are presented on this history site.

https://www.bbc.com/news/world-europe-17217954
This timeline of Croatia's history begins in 1918.

http://croatia.eu/page.php?lang=2&id=13
This Croatia information site includes an in-depth history section.

http://www.icty.org/en/about/what-former-yugoslavia
This UN page for the International Criminal Tribunal for the Former Yugoslavia details the conflicts that followed the breakup of Yugoslavia.

https://www.travelchannel.com/destinations/croatia/articles/crash-course-in-croatias-history
This travel site provides a quick, easy overview of Croatia's history.

https://whc.unesco.org/en/list/97
This page about the Historical Complex of Split with the Palace of Diocletian includes a video and photographs.

GOVERNMENT

Flags wave at the entrance to the Croatian
Parliament Building in Zagreb.

3

THE REPUBLIC OF CROATIA IS A parliamentary democracy with a president as head of state. The December 22, 1990, constitution defines Croatia as an indivisible, democratic, and social state structured on the separation of executive, judicial, and legislative powers.

The introduction to the constitution sets forth the "inalienable and indivisible, non-transferable and perpetual right of the Croatian nation to self-determination and state sovereignty." It establishes the historical foundation of the nation based on its various manifestations over time, beginning in the seventh century CE with the formation of the Croatian principalities.

THE CONSTITUTION

At the time of the breakup of Yugoslavia, it was necessary to establish the independent nation of Croatia by drawing up a new constitution. This document spells out the citizens' basic rights and responsibilities, describes the structure of the government, and details the rule of law. The constitution has held up, with the addition of several amendments.

The most recent amendment, as of 2019, was added in 2013. The country held a referendum on the question of same-sex marriage. Voters were asked, "Are you in favor of the constitution of the Republic of Croatia being amended with a provision stating that marriage is matrimony between a woman and a man?" In this case, a yes vote would constitutionally prevent the legalization of same-sex marriage in Croatia.

The Croatian Parliament adopted the Constitution of the Republic of Croatia on December 22, 1990. Because of the date, it's popularly known as the "Christmas Constitution." The document remains in effect, though parliament amended it in 1997, 2000, 2001, 2010, and 2013.

Being a strongly Catholic country, it was perhaps not surprising that Croatia passed the amendment. However, only 37.9 percent of eligible voters voted.

Nevertheless, as a result of that referendum, Croatia's constitution defines marriage solely as a union between a woman and a man, effectively prohibiting same-sex marriage. Article 61 reads, "The family shall enjoy special protection of the state. Marriage is a living union between a woman and a man. Marriage and legal relations in marriage, common-law marriage and the family shall be regulated by law."

THE EXECUTIVE BRANCH

The president is the chief of state. He or she is elected by an absolute-majority popular vote (in two rounds if necessary) for a five-year term. The president is eligible for a second term. In 2015, Kolinda Grabar-Kitarović

Kolinda Grabar-Kitarović is sworn in as president of Croatia during a ceremony in Zagreb on February 15, 2015.

FRANJO TUDJMAN

The founder and first president of the Republic of Croatia, Franjo Tudjman, was born on May 14, 1922, in Veliko Trgovišće, in northwest Croatia. At the age of nineteen, he joined the antifascist partisan movement to fight against the Ustaše regime. In 1960, Tudjman became the youngest general in the Yugoslav army. Two years later, he left the military to study history and eventually headed the Institute for the History of the Workers' Movement. Tudjman was kicked out of the Communist Party in 1967 for questioning the government's figures on the victims of the Ustaše puppet government during World War II. In the early 1970s, he was jailed for three years for being a part of a movement to get more independence for Croatia.

In February 1981, for speaking against the communist system during interviews with foreign journalists, Tudjman was sentenced to a three-year prison term and prohibited from engaging in public activity for a further five years. In 1989, Tudjman founded the Hrvatska Demokratska Zajednica (HDZ), or Croatian Democratic Union, and became its president. After his party's victory in the first Croatian democratic elections, he was elected president in 1990. He was reelected in the presidential election of June 1997.

Tudjman's popularity declined in later years. After he came to power, Croatians became poorer, and unemployment hit an all-time high of 20.8 percent in December 1999. His government was accused of corruption, cronyism, and inefficiency, and the Croatian political system was described by observers as "nominally democratic." Tudjman's nationalistic beliefs, which won him the presidency in 1990, led to policies that fueled the civil war with ethnic Serbs in Croatia. The 1991–1995 hostilities resulted in the loss of 250,000 lives, and the economy suffered.

In a decade as president of Croatia, Tudjman imposed one-man rule, which means he had the final say in parliamentary and judicial matters. Tudjman's near-dictatorial rule ended on December 10, 1999, with his death after an illness.

Prime Minister Andrej Plenković speaks at a campaign rally for the European Parliament elections in Zagreb in May 2019.

(b. 1968) became the president. She is Croatia's first woman president and was also the youngest, at age forty-six when she was first elected. From 2008 to 2011, she served as Croatia's ambassador to the United States.

The president appoints the prime minister, who is the head of government. The prime minister names a Council of Ministers, or cabinet. The prime minister is usually the leader of the majority party. In 2016, President Grabar-Kitarović appointed Andrej Plenković (b. 1970) as prime minister. Both executives are members of the Croatian Democratic Union (HDZ), a conservative, pro-European, center-right political party. At this writing in 2019, it holds fifty-five seats in the legislature, the most of any party.

THE LEGISLATURE

Croatia has a single-house legislature, or parliament, the Sabor. From 1990 until 2000, there were two houses, similar to the Congress of the United States, but a constitutional amendment in 2000 did away with the second house.

The Sabor passes laws, proposes constitutional reform, adopts the national budget, and decides on matters of defense and sovereignty. Members are selected from party lists, and the number from each party is decided by popular vote.

There are 151 seats in the Sabor. Of those, 140 members are elected from multiseat electoral districts. Croatia has twelve electoral districts, or territorial subdivisions. Ten of those lie within Croatia itself, with each providing fourteen representatives to the Sabor, for a total of 140. The remaining eleven seats come from the other two electoral districts—District 11 represents citizens living abroad, with three members, and District 12 is for national minority groups, such as ethnic Serbs, providing eight members.

All members are elected by popular vote for a four-year term. At this writing, the next election was scheduled for December 2020.

The Supreme Court building is located in Zagreb.

THE JUDICIARY

Croatia has a three-tiered legal system. The highest judicial authority in Croatia, as in the United States, is the Supreme Court, to which appeals may be made against decisions by county courts. Justices are appointed by the National Judicial Council and serve until age seventy.

The second judicial level is made up of the county courts, and the third level is the municipal (town) courts.

Questions relating to the constitution are referred to the Constitutional Court, whose eleven judges sit for eight-year terms.

This map shows the twenty regional administrative districts in Croatia.

LOCAL GOVERNMENT

Croatia is divided into twenty *županijas* (zhoo-PAH-nee-yahs), or regional counties, plus the capital city of Zagreb. County boundaries are designed to reflect local, historic, and economic considerations. Županijas were introduced in the tenth century as a more advanced form of structuring the Croatian state.

In the 1990 constitution, they were reintroduced, and two years later, the Croatian parliament passed a law to determine the boundaries of the counties, towns, and municipalities. Each county acts with a great measure of autonomy in matters of local administration and local government. Similarly, the 428 municipalities and 128 town councils in Croatia are largely self-governing.

FOREIGN RELATIONS

In the twenty-first century, Croatia has sought to forge closer relations with both the European Union (EU) and the North Atlantic Treaty Organization (NATO). In February 2003, Croatia applied for EU membership, and in April 2004, the European Commission agreed to open EU negotiations with Croatia, but only if Croatia cooperated with the ongoing war crimes investigation in The Hague, Netherlands. Talks finally got under way in October 2005 after information from the Croatian government helped in the arrest of indicted war criminal General Ante Gotovina by Spanish police in the Canary Islands.

In 2000, Croatia joined the Partnership for Peace program as a step toward becoming a full NATO member. In May 2003, the United States joined Croatia,

Albania, and Macedonia to sign the Adriatic Charter, in which the three Balkan countries pledged their commitment to NATO values. In 2008, the Adriatic Charter expanded to include two new countries, Bosnia and Herzegovina and Montenegro. Croatia was invited to join NATO at the NATO Summit in April 2008 and became a full member of the alliance in April 2009. In 2013, Croatia became the twenty-eighth member state of the European Union.

Croatia has been a member of the United Nations since 1992 and has contributed troops to various UN operations, including those in Haiti, Cyprus, Georgia, Ethiopia, Eritrea, and Kashmir.

Croatia has good relations with the United States. The US Department of Defense provides Croatia with military assistance in the form of training, equipment, and education, and was a source of support during the Croatian War of Independence. In addition, the United States has provided humanitarian assistance of more than $27 million.

INTERNET LINKS

https://croatia.eu/page.php?lang=2&id=14
The constitution and the government are the subject of this Croatian website.

https://hr.usembassy.gov
The site of the US Embassy in Croatia provides information on the two countries' relationship.

https://www.usud.hr/sites/default/files/dokumenti/The_ consolidated_text_of_the_Constitution_of_the_Republic_of_ Croatia_as_of_15_January_2014.pdf
An English-language PDF of Croatia's constitution, valid as of 2014, is available on the site of the Croatian Constitutional Court.

https://vlada.gov.hr/en
The government of Croatia provides news and information on an English-language version of its official website.

ECONOMY

The European Union welcomes Croatia as a new member in July 2013 in Brussels, Belgium.

4

F OLLOWING THE BREAK-UP OF Yugoslavia and the communist system in 1990, Croatia began converting its economy to market-based capitalism. The transition, however, was greatly impeded by the war during that decade. War damages cost the newly independent country some $37 billion, leaving it and its people quite impoverished. Industry suffered, and unemployment was high. In such an atmosphere, corruption and economic crime took root.

Just as Croatia was climbing out of that hole, however, the global economic crisis of 2008—2009 hit, once again slowing progress. In more recent years, the economy has been doing better, but it is not yet on solid ground. Unemployment has remained high throughout the country's years of independence and remains a key challenge for the government. Croatia has also not privatized at as fast a rate as many other former communist countries, and the government still retains a massive stake in the economy and is the country's biggest employer.

Despite these setbacks, Croatia remains one of the wealthiest of the former Yugoslav republics, with average national incomes on a level with many mid-income countries. Croatia joined the European Union (EU) in 2013 after a ten-year accession process. Since then, the country has seen

In 2019, the minimum monthly net wage in Croatia was raised from $415.38 (370 euros) to $453.55 (€404).

WHAT IS GDP?

Gross domestic product (GDP) is a measure of a country's total production. The number reflects the total value of goods and services produced over one year. Economists use it to determine whether a country's economy is growing or contracting. Growth is good, while a falling GDP means trouble. Dividing the GDP by the number of people in the country determines the GDP per capita (per person). This number provides an indication of a country's average standard of living—the higher the better.

In 2017, the GDP per capita in Croatia was approximately $24,700. That figure ranked Croatia 81st out of 229 countries listed by the CIA World Factbook. *For comparison, the United States that year was number 19, with a GDP per capita of $59,500. Croatia's neighbor Slovenia did better at number 58, with $34,500, but most of Croatia's Balkan neighbors were much lower—with Serbia at number 111 with a GDP per capita of $15,100; Bosnia and Herzogovina at 122 with $12,800; and Albania at 125 with $12,500.*

its exports grow from below 40 percent of the gross domestic product (GDP) in 2008 to above 50 percent in 2018.

INDUSTRY

Industry is one of Croatia's biggest economic sectors, employing 27.3 percent of all workers. The sector accounts for about 26 percent of the country's GDP and includes key industries such as shipbuilding, petroleum refining, machine tools manufacture, chemical products, construction materials, and food and drinks.

Construction has, for many years, been a stable industry in Croatia. From the 1960s to the 1980s, this sector grew, building hotels and other tourist-related facilities. However, construction almost stopped completely during the 1991–1995 war.

Since then, the building industry has revived, with the need for national reconstruction, including new housing and the reconstruction of heritage sites, supported by international donations. From 2014 to 2020, the EU invested $16 billion to develop the transport, education, research and innovation, and

SHIPBUILDING

Croatia, located far from the world's major shipping lanes, was once the third-largest shipbuilder in the world. In the 1960s, only Japan and South Korea produced more and bigger ships. Ships built in Croatia were well known for their quality and innovative design solutions.

The country's tradition of shipbuilding goes back over one thousand years. The only interruption came during the sixteenth to eighteenth centuries, when Venetian rule in Dalmatia forbade the construction of ships and stripped Croatia's coastal timber to support Venice's own shipbuilding industry.

During the 1960s and 1970s, Croatia constructed large ships for clients, mostly in the United States and Scandinavia. By the end of the 1990s, after being interrupted by war, Croatia's shipbuilding industry began to regain its former prominence.

In recent years, however, the industry in Croatia has not been faring well. China leads the world in shipbuilding, and Japan and South Korea still dominate as well. Since 2011, Croatia's shipyards have not been profitable. Some builders have been unable to meet customer demands and have not been able to stand up to international competition. Orders have fallen off precipitously.

Croatia's largest shipbuilding yards are partly owned by the government. Although the state has poured money into trying to save—and then sell—state-owned shipyards, efforts have yielded little success. Finding a solution to building a sustainable shipbuilding sector will surely help Croatia's economy.

Uljanik, a Croatian company, began operating this shipyard in Pula in 1856.

energy sectors. It plans to allocate another $10.4 billion from 2021 to 2027. The Croatian government, likewise, has commissioned construction projects to develop infrastructure. Thanks to the skills and the relatively low cost of Croatian workers, an increasing number of international competitive contracts are being won by Croatia.

Trade is beginning to play a growing role in the economy, with exports topping $13 billion in recent years. Much of Croatia's trade is with neighboring countries such as Italy, Slovenia, and Bosnia and Herzegovina, where products such as transport equipment, textiles, fuel, and food are exported.

AGRICULTURE AND FORESTRY

Agriculture plays a small role in today's Croatian economy. Farming employs roughly 1.9 percent of the working population and contributes 3.7 percent of the GDP per year.

There are 7.4 million acres (3 million hectares) of agricultural land, of which 62 percent is cultivated. The remainder is pasture land. Most of the cultivated

Merchants sell produce at the outdoor Dolac Market in Zagreb.

area is found within the fertile Pannonian region, which covers some 55 percent of the country's total surface area and produces most of its food and farm products. Croatian farmers raise wheat, corn, sugar beets, olives, potatoes, and beans, in addition to dairy farming and livestock rearing. Fishing is also a growth industry on Croatia's Dalmatian coast, with a huge recent surge in demand from East Asia.

Of Croatia's extensive forests, three-quarters are state-owned, with the rest in private hands. The rich resource of high-quality timber has fed a growing wood-processing and furniture industry. As forest resources decline in the rest of the world, Croatia's relatively cheap and plentiful hardwoods are very attractive to the United States and northern Europe. The Croatian common oak, renowned for its beautiful color and hardness, is in great demand when made into solid period furniture and high-quality flooring—such products are almost totally exported and bring in badly needed US dollars and Euros.

TOURISM

With its beautiful coastline and fascinating history, Croatia has been a popular tourist destination for decades, and tourism is an important source of foreign revenue. However, tourists only visit in peacetime and when the world economy is strong, so Croatia's tourist industry is dependent on these external factors. Until 1990, tourism was Croatia's largest source of foreign currency and a major source of employment.

The war brought about a sudden end to the tourist boom and to a major industry. Although Croatia has been at peace since 1995, lingering hostilities in neighboring Balkan countries didn't help matters. In 1999, the NATO bombing of Serbia caused tourism in Croatia to nosedive again, with newly renovated hotels left empty and newly trained staff seeming unnecessary before they had even begun work.

Today, however, the Balkans are at peace, and tourism remains a strong and growing part of the economy. Croatia is regularly ranked among the top twenty vacation destinations in the world, especially among European travelers. In 2018, Croatia received 18.4 million tourists, contributing 20 percent of the

The medieval city of Dubrovnik, a UNESCO World Heritage site, has long been a popular tourist attraction. In recent years, a new kind of tourist has been flocking to the city. Fans of the blockbuster TV series Game of Thrones *come to see the locations of scenes filmed in Dubrovnik, such as those that were set in the Westerosi capital of King's Landing.*

Game of Thrones isn't the only fantasy to make use of Dubrovnik's charming sites. Parts of The Last Jedi, *the eighth episode in the* Star Wars *saga, were filmed there as well. The 2018 film* Robin Hood, *produced by Leonardo DiCaprio, and a new James Bond movie were also shot in the scenic city.*

While some worry that the older, historic parts of Dubrovnik can't handle the masses, other locals admit that the "Hollywood tourism" has benefited the city economically.

country's GDP. With the seacoast playing such a major role in attracting visitors, the high season is July and August. Such an emphasis on seasonality, however, means many tourism jobs are temporary. Some 45 percent of workers employed in the tourism industry are temporary workers, by far the highest rate in the EU. Compounding that problem is the difficulty that the industry has in filling those positions. In 2019, the Ministry of Tourism announced the government would invest some $1.69 billion in building up the industry, mostly in the construction of new accommodations.

ENERGY SOURCES

As people and industry became poorer after 1991, the consumption of energy decreased. This led to a small increase in the export of energy, mostly in the form of liquid fuel and natural gas by pipeline to Serbia, Bosnia and Herzegovina, and Slovenia.

Croatia is fortunate to have a relative abundance of oil and natural gas. Nevertheless, domestic sources only provide for about 40 percent of Croatia's needs, and it's been necessary to import the rest. Plans exist to exploit these resources further so that the country can import less oil and gas from abroad.

A liquified natural gas terminal on the island of Krk serves as an energy port for the country.

The Croatian petrochemical industry is established on the island of Krk, an ideal entry point for crude oil, gas, and petroleum products that are bound for Central and Eastern European countries. This is largely because of the qualities of Krk's deepwater port and its proximity to Central Europe. Prospects for developing both the domestic energy sector and the trade in energy for re-export are bright.

WORKING LIFE

The average monthly wage, adjusted for cost of living in Croatia, was $1,782 in 2017. That translates to about $21,384 annually. This figure was one of the highest in the Balkan region and good for a developing former communist country. The national currency, the kuna, is tied to the euro. After joining the EU in 2013, Croatia was on track to join the Eurozone, and therefore adopt the euro as its currency. As of 2019, it planned to switch over from the kuna to the euro in 2020.

Croatia has had high unemployment for many years, with 12.4 percent of the labor force recorded as being out of work in 2017, falling from 15 percent in 2016. Inflation (the annual rise of the cost of goods and services) has slowed from a relatively high 6.1 percent in 2008 to about 1.1 percent in 2017. Nevertheless, it's a major problem that continues to affect the individual wealth of families and the country's attempts to improve the economy.

INFRASTRUCTURE

Most land routes from Western Europe to the Aegean Sea and Turkish straits pass through Croatian territory, making the country a key staging point for road and rail traffic. Croatia has a well-developed highway and state road network, in relatively good condition. The country has 17,888 miles (28,788 km) of roads—including 540 miles (870 km) of expressways—of which 12,420 miles (20,000 km) are paved. The highways mainly connect the capital, Zagreb, to other main cities and towns. Most highways are tolled.

A toll gate marks the entrance to a highway tunnel in Učka, in Istria.

Croatia has an extensive railway network, with 1,722 miles (2,772 km) of railroad track, of which 611 miles (983 km) are electrified. The entire rail system is operated by the government-owned Croatian Railways. Because of Croatia's unusual shape, regions such as Istria and Dubrovnik can only be reached by rail track that passes through neighboring countries, such as Slovenia and Bosnia and Herzegovina. Two trains connect Zagreb and Belgrade every day, and four trains run daily between Zagreb and Budapest. There are also direct lines to and from Austria, Czech Republic, Switzerland, Germany, Hungary, and Slovenia.

The main seaports of Rijeka, Split, and Ploĉe are well connected to the interior and to Zagreb.

Croatia has three main international airports located in Zagreb, Split, and Dubrovnik. Other important airports are located in Zadar, Rijeka (on the island of Krk), Osijek, and Pula. Croatian Airlines is the national airline and flag carrier.

River transportation is generally less important than in the past, except on Croatia's major river, the Sava, which is the subject of an international plan to link the Danube and Sava Rivers and construct an inland port at the Croatian city of Osijek.

INTERNET LINKS

https://croatia.eu/page.php?lang=2&id=15
Various aspects of the Croatian economy are covered on this site.

https://www.worldbank.org/en/country/croatia/overview
The World Bank offers a quick overview of Croatia's economy.

ENVIRONMENT

Only about thirty to fifty Eurasian lynx remain in Croatia, where road accidents, poaching, and a lack of food are major threats.

5

HISTORICALLY, CROATIA HAS HAD little heavy industry compared with many Eastern European countries, which has meant that its coasts, rivers, and forests have remained relatively unpolluted.

According to the EU, waste management, water management, and air quality are the most important environmental issues facing Croatia.

Nevertheless, problems remain. Croatia's forests are threatened with damage from acid rain caused by emissions from metalworking, factories, and refineries in neighboring countries. And although the seas around the Adriatic coast are among the cleanest in Europe, heavy fishing over many years has drastically reduced the fish population, and tourism in the coastal areas has put additional pressure on Croatia's marine life.

Croatia relies on traditional sources—oil, gas, and coal—for much of its energy. One hundred percent of the population has access to electricity. The government has been slow to develop an integrated, sustainable energy program. However, in recent years, wind farms for generating electricity have been catching on. The first wind farm was installed on the island of Pag in 2004, and in 2006, another farm opened near Šibenik.

In 2018, Croatia's state-run power utility HEP announced that it aims to boost renewable energy from 35 percent to 50 percent of its total capacity. Over the coming years, it intends to invest 1 billion Croatian kuna ($153.96 million) a year on average until 2030. As part of the plan, it will upgrade hydroelectric power plants, build new ones, and invest in other renewable sources, including solar and wind farms.

AIR POLLUTION

Croatia suffered a lot of air pollution in the communist era, before its independence. In 1996, industrial carbon dioxide emissions totaled 19 million tons (17.5 million metric tons), which rose to 21 million tons (19 million metric tons) in 2009. In recent years, the country has made a huge effort to meet international guidelines on industrial pollution, which was key to its being accepted into the EU. In 2005, the Croatian parliament adopted the Air Protection Act to help reduce the effects of industrial damage to the environment. Environmental management has also become more decentralized, thereby empowering local government bodies to decide local environmental policy.

WATER RESOURCES

More than 99 percent of Croatians have access to improved drinking water—higher than most countries in the region. Most household water comes from groundwater sources. In the towns, every household has access to safe drinking water.

Industrial air pollution remains a problem in Croatia.

Croatia has plenty of rainfall in the winter months, and in inland areas, almost as much rainfall occurs in the summer. Croatia also draws water from a number of major river systems, including the Danube, Drava, and Sava in the Danube River basin, and the Neretva on the Adriatic coast. For these reasons, water shortages have never been of concern, and the country is green and fertile for most of the year.

All water is owned and distributed by the government. Water is managed by region and based around major water courses and hydrographic areas. Croatia has signed international agreements with its neighbors in the management of the Danube River system, which affects Hungary, Bosnia and Herzegovina, and Slovenia.

Many of Croatia's rivers and watercourses pass through forested areas, and the management of these wetland forests has been key in preserving the water system. The forests and watercourses play an interdependent role

LAND MINES

Land mines are a weapon of war that keep on killing long after the war is over. In 1997, a UN treaty banning land mines was signed by 80 percent of the world's countries. Among those nations that refused to sign the treaty are the United States, China, Russia, India, and Pakistan. Unfortunately, the treaty came too late to help Croatia, where land mines saw extensive use during the War of Independence.

Though the war ended in 1995, Croatia still has a huge problem with uncleared, unexploded mines. During the four-year war, as many as two million land mines were laid by both sides in the conflict, affecting up to 8 percent of Croatia's territory. Many of the mines were laid in disputed, ethnically mixed areas, mainly where Croatia borders Bosnia and Herzegovina, in the Krajina region, and also around eastern Slavonia, near the Serbian border. This has given Croatia one of the worst land mine problems in Europe, and several hundred people have been killed by hidden mines since the end of hostilities.

Between 1991 and 2013, 509 people were killed by mines and another 1,466 were wounded. The casualty rate has fallen in recent years as minefields have been mapped and fenced off. Sadly, a large number of the casualties have been children, who are less aware of the problem. The mine problem has also affected the country's tourist industry. A Dutch tourist was badly injured in 2003 on the island of Vis.

The Croatian government has undertaken a massive campaign to educate Croatians about the terrible dangers of the unexploded mines. The government has also put into action a demining program, carried out by hundreds of bomb disposal experts, demining machines, and detection dogs. Large areas of Croatia have been cleared of mines, with 16.5 square miles (42 sq km) of land cleared in 2001 alone. The Croatian military also destroyed its stockpile of almost two hundred thousand antipersonnel mines in 2002.

Experts said a UN deadline of 2019 for being completely free of mines could not be met, not by Croatia nor any of the other Balkan countries. Rocky, forested, and mountainous areas, which prevent the use of demining machines, posed particular challenges to the mission.

in preserving the ecosystem, with the rivers sustaining the forests and the tree roots, in turn, helping maintain river banks by preventing soil erosion.

Flooding is an occasional problem, both in the mountainous areas along the coast and in the Danube basin. However, Croatia has a long history of managing both problems through creating flood plains around the Danube and Sava Rivers and constructing sills in torrential riverbeds.

The waters around Croatia's coast are of high quality and of a very good standard for swimming—good news for the country's tourism industry.

WASTE MANAGEMENT

Managing the country's ever-increasing amounts of trash has become one of the most pressing problems in modern Croatia. Systems have yet to be set

Upon joining the EU in 2013, Croatia also became part of the Natura 2000 network—a Europe-wide ecological network of nature conservation areas. All EU member states have designated Natura 2000 sites to help conserve the rare habitats and species present in their territory. In Croatia, more than one-third of its land area was selected to be enfolded into the network.

The measure should prove to be helpful for Croatia's rich biodiversity and three bio-geographical regions. The laws and protections of the Natura 2000 community will now cover Croatia's wildlife in these protected regions.

up to recycle household waste, and there are few official disposal sites. The government plans to introduce the organized collection of all household waste so that every home is covered by 2025 and is planning to set up twenty-one county waste management centers with treatment plants and landfills. The Zagreb waste management center will include an incinerator and a wastewater plant for dealing with sewage sludge.

FORESTS AND WOODLANDS

Forests and woodlands cover about 46 percent of the Croatian land surface, making Croatia one of the most densely forested countries in Europe. Roughly 77 percent of the forest land is state owned. The government manages this national resource through sixteen separate forest administrations. Currently 6 percent of Croatia's forest land area is protected, and the authorities intend to expand their conservation efforts.

Deciduous trees make up 84 percent of the forest, and coniferous species make up 16 percent. Birch and oak are the most common species of tree found in Croatia, as well as hornbeam, fir, spruce, and pine. Approximately 1,235 acres (500 hectares) of forest are cut down each year, but more than 2,471 acres (1,000 ha) of forest are replaced, so the annual increase of forest easily exceeds the logging that takes place. In recent years, more forest land has become privately owned, and private owners have been less interested in

From a helicopter, the lush wooded tip of the Pelješac Peninsula can be seen.

managing the trees in a sustainable way, leading to some deterioration in the conditions of some forests.

Croatia has hot, dry summers, and any kind of fire easily catches hold in these conditions. In most of the national parks, starting a fire is forbidden. However, every year, forest fires destroy between 7,413 and 168,031 acres (3,000 and 68,000 ha) of forests in the coastal areas. The majority of fires start on privately owned, disused agricultural land. These forest fires do a lot of damage to local resources, wildlife, and agriculture, and they damage tourist and recreational facilities. The government has spent a lot of money and hours dealing with the fires, and the country's fire prevention systems—firebreaks and forest roads for easy access by firefighting teams—are in need of modernization.

Predictions are that climate change will likely increase the incidence of forst fires in Croatia, particularly in the southern regions.

People enjoy the waters of Krka National Park, one of eight national parks in Croatia.

PROTECTED AREAS

Croatia has many national parks and protected areas. In 2003, the Croatian government created an administrative body, the State Institute for Nature Protection, to be responsible for maintaining the country's protected areas and national parks. About 2,849 square miles (4,584 sq km) of the land are protected nature reserves.

There are eight national parks in Croatia. These include the Brijuni group of islands, the Kornati archipelago, Krka National Park, the island of Mljet,

The Ecological and Fisheries Protection Zone (ZERP) is a protected fishing area of 9,216 square miles (23,870 sq km) in the waters around Croatia's coastline and islands. Introduced in 2008, the zone is internationally recognized and is enforced by Croatia's European Union neighbors. Croatia created the zone to restrict fishing and exploitation of its waters by neighboring countries' fishing fleets, especially from Italy. At one time, Italian boats were catching ten times as many fish as local Croatian fishing ships. Croatians of every political persuasion support the creation of the zone. The preservation of the coastline and coastal waters is seen as key to developing the economically important tourist industry.

Paklenica, Plitvice Lakes National Park, and National Park Sjeverni Velebit. Another protected area, Risnjak National Park, is in the most mountainous and heavily forested region of the country, on the Croatian—Slovenian border.

Plitvice Lakes is Croatia's oldest national park, gaining this status in 1949. The park is home to some 126 recorded species of birds, of which 70 breed in the area. The most popular Croatian national park is Plitvice Lakes, followed by Krka, Brijuni, and Paklenica.

There are also eleven nature parks. Nature parks are protected areas that are of less conservation value than a national park. The parks include Učka Mountain Park in Istria, the 88-square-mile (228 sq km) Medvednica Mountain Park, Kopački Rit, Lonjsko Polje, and Biokovo, which preserves the second-highest mountain range in Croatia, near the Dalmatian coast.

A part of Kopački Rit is designated as a special zoological reserve. Around 260 bird species nest there, including wild geese and ducks, great white egrets, white storks, black storks, white-tailed eagles, terns, kingfishers, and green woodpeckers. Many other birds stop in the area while migrating from Central to Southern Europe during the winter months. The area is also famous for its many mammal inhabitants, including red deer, roe deer, wild boar, wild cat, pine marten, stone marten, weasel, and otter.

In the Medvednica Mountain Park, ninety-two species of plants are on the endangered list, and twenty species are protected by law. The protected plants include the pyramidal orchid, the downy birch, the leopard's bane, the lesser butterfly orchid, and the Balkan daphne.

A wild boar is at home in the Kopački Rit Nature Park, near the border with Serbia.

ENDANGERED SPECIES

In Croatia, the International Union for Conservation of Nature (IUCN) Red List includes as vulnerable the Eurasian otter, garden dormouse, and seven species of bats. Other threatened species include the Adriatic sturgeon and the Mediterranean monk seal, both of which are sometimes found in Croatian waters.

Various conservation projects have been established throughout the country, especially in the mountains and islands along the Adriatic coast. On the island of Cres, a sanctuary has been set up to protect the small numbers of local griffon vultures—some of the few to survive in Eastern Europe. Weighing up to 30 pounds (13 kg), with an average wingspan of 9 feet (2.7 m), the griffon is one of the largest flying birds in the world. Griffons tend to feed on the carcasses of dead sheep or domestic animals. A conservation project has also been set up at Miljacka Cave in Krka National Park to halt the decline of the long-fingered bat.

The endangered Mediterranean monk seal can be found on the small island of Šćedro, off the south coast of Hvar, and on the uninhabited island of Brusnik.

The griffon vulture is an impressive-looking bird of prey.

WOLVES

According to a 2014 report, there were between 136 and 199 wolves in Croatia, divided into roughly 40 to 50 packs. In 1990, there were as few as 50 wolves in Croatia, but the numbers had increased to 130 to 170 by 2000. The wolves live mainly in the hilly and mountainous areas close to the Adriatic coast, especially Gorski Kotar, Lika, and Dalmatia. Some of the wolf packs cross the border with Slovenia or Bosnia and Herzegovina, where there is no monitoring of the population.

Humans pose the most serious threat to the survival of the wolf in Croatia. Road construction fragments their natural habitat, farmers shoot wolves to protect their livestock, and poachers continue to kill wolves for their pelts. Killing wolves for any reason, except for an emergency, is now outlawed in the country.

In 1995, the government declared wolves a protected species, and since 2000, the numbers of wolves reported killed have decreased. This may be due to greater public awareness of the plight of wolves and perhaps a reluctance to report the death of a wolf for fear of being fined.

Since 2013, bears are also a strictly protected species, similar to wolves. Lynxes also may not be hunted.

The Mediterranean monk seal is nearly extinct in Croatia.

These elegant seals grow to a length of up to 8 feet (2.4 m) and weigh up to 650 pounds (300 kg). Recent estimates suggest there are as few as twenty-five of these beautiful creatures still living in Croatian territory.

The Eurasian lynx was long considered extinct in Slovenia and Croatia. However, a resettlement project that began in 1973 successfully reintroduced the lynx to the Slovenian Alps and Croatia's Plitvice Lakes National Park and Risnjak National Park.

The lynx is the most endangered mammal species in Croatia, with a very small population. Because there are so few left, there are problems with inbreeding, and authorities are considering bringing in new animals to broaden the gene pool. Although the lynx is protected by law, the national park authorities do arrange lynx-spotting trips.

**http://ec.europa.eu/environment/life/project/Projects/
index.cfm?fuseaction=home.showFile&rep=file&fil=CROWOLFCON_
final_report.pdf**
This report offers a history of Croatians' changing attitudes
toward wolves.

**http://ec.europa.eu/environment/nature/natura2000/
index_en.htm**
This European Commission site provides information on Natura 2000.

https://www.eea.europa.eu/countries-and-regions/croatia
The European Environment Agency provides fact sheets relevant
to Croatia.

**https://www.greeneuropeanjournal.eu/what-does-the-eu-bring-to
-croatias-environment**
This article details the steps Croatia must take to meet EU standards.

**https://www.nytimes.com/2018/04/04/lens/the-endless-war-of
-land-mines-in-the-balkans.html**
This article discusses the problem of old land mines in the
Balkan region.

https://www.total-croatia.com/environment-in-croatia
This site has a wide range of environmental information with links,
photos, and videos.

https://www.total-croatia.com/national-parks-of-croatia
The nation's national parks and nature reserves are presented with
photos and videos.

CROATIANS

A girl attends church dressed in a traditional folk costume on Homeland Thanksgiving Day in the village of Štitar.

6

N THE EARLY 1990s, THE CROATIAN War of Independence and similar conflicts in neighboring states caused a great movement of people across new national boundaries. Most movement was inspired by fear and involved people moving from an area where they were an ethnic minority to an area where they were the majority.

For most of the last century, the population of Croatia was increasing, but this trend was reversed during the war. Many ethnic Serbs living in Croatia fled to neighboring Serbia. Also, some Croatians fled abroad, seeking a better life in a safer country.

ETHNIC GROUPS

Before 1990, 78 percent of Croatians were ethnic Croat—that is, they saw themselves as Croat by heritage and spoke Croatian. Most were Roman Catholics and shared a common view of history and origin. About 12 percent of Croatians were ethnic Serbs, but many left Croatia during the period of violence and war. Some have moved back to Croatia since, but now the Serb community is smaller than its prewar size, making up about 4.4 percent of the population. With people from other ethnic

A custom developed among Croatian expats for emigrants to take some ancestral soil with them and, when the time comes, to be buried with it. This inspired the poet Drago Ivanišević (1907–1981) to write, "As a Croat I am brother of all men. Wherever I go Croatia is with me."

The Romani, or Roma, people are one of the smallest ethnic groups in Croatia. These traditionally itinerant people, originally from northern India, settled in the country more than six hundred years ago. Today, they are concentrated mostly in Croatia's northern regions.

The 2011 census put the Romani population at 16,675, but the real number of Romani in Croatia may be higher, as Romani often do not declare their ethnicity for fear of discrimination. These people are sometimes called Gypsies, but that term, often associated with illegal activities, is now considered derogatory. Romani  *are spread throughout Eastern Europe and beyond. In most countries, as in Croatia, they tend to be marginalized, poor, and poorly educated.*

About half the Romani in Croatia are Roman Catholics, 14 percent are Eastern Orthodox, and 30 percent are Muslims. Romani are represented politically through proportional representation in the Croatian legislature.

groups having fled the country during the 1990s, today the Croatians are an even more dominant group, making up 90.4 percent of the population.

Other groups in Croatia include small communities of Bosnian Muslims, Hungarians, Slovenes, Italians, Czechs, Albanians, and Jews. The new constitution and legislative structure try to ensure that such groups are proportionally represented. Their rights are constitutionally guaranteed under the final settlements that ended the hostilities of the 1990s.

Officially, there are approximately 4.27 million Croatians, both ethnic Croatians and minorities, living in Croatia.

THE CROATIAN DIASPORA

It is difficult to estimate accurately how many Croatians live abroad. Since the wars of the 1990s, many Croatians have fled abroad as refugees, and some have settled in their new country and become naturalized citizens; others have returned to Croatia. Most estimates suggest that up to 2 million Croatians live in some forty countries around the world. Large numbers of ethnic Croats live in other states in the former Yugoslavia, especially in Bosnia and Herzegovina, where they make up about 15.4 percent of the population. Elsewhere in Europe, it is estimated there are at least 227,500 people of Croatian descent living in Germany, while a large number also live in Austria.

Overseas, the United States is home to the largest number of people of full or partial Croatian descent (over 408,000 in 2017), mostly in Ohio, Pennsylvania, Illinois, and California. Large numbers of Croatians have also moved to Australia and Canada, and significant numbers of people claim Croatian descent in Chile and Argentina. Overseas Croatians may retain their citizenship, unless they renounce it, and may vote in parliamentary elections from a special list that is internationally distributed.

The Croatian diaspora has a long history. In the fourteenth and fifteenth centuries, many young men left Croatia to pursue higher education in Italy and elsewhere. Some returned, but many did not. When Ottoman forces invaded Croatia in the fifteenth century, some 400,000 Croats left for Italy, Austria, Hungary, Slovakia, and Romania. Wherever they went, they preserved their language, customs, and culture. In the southern Italian province of Molise, a group of wholly Croatian villages may be found.

Croats were also among the earliest settlers in the New World, with communities in Canada, the southern United States, and Mexico. Today, in Canada, thousands of Croats gather each year, dressed in national costumes, to celebrate the Canadian Croatian Folklore Festival.

A statue of Saint Jerome graces the front of the Croatian Embassy in Washington, DC. Saint Jerome was born in Strido, Dalmatia (Croatia), in 347 CE.

In 1991, these Croatian civilians packed up their belongings to flee from the fighting of the civil war.

The diaspora was fueled by problems at home and attractions overseas. Following the example of Croatian Christian leaders who fled the Turks and prospered in Europe, Croatian Muslims later fled the Austro-Hungarian Empire and moved to Turkey, where they were welcomed. From 1900 to 1914, emigration from Croatia was so massive that it was predicted that it would not survive as a nation. Between World War I and World War II, Croatia remained divided and poor. At that time, some 100,000 Croatians were attracted to the opportunities in South America and the mines of Belgium.

Even after World War II, emigration continued with the blessing of the communist authorities because it reduced unemployment at home, eased political pressure, and was the major source of hard currency for the new country. About 800,000 Croats left to work in other European countries at this time. Most never returned, and many joined in a secondary migration to

Australia, Canada, and the United States. Their money was sent to relatives in Croatia and helped build the economy, including one of the largest tourist industries in the world.

SOCIAL HIERARCHIES

Like other Europeans, Croats are susceptible to the divisions and injustices created by the growth of social hierarchy in their society. In the past, the peasant classes lived in small stone houses, which blended into the land on which they worked, and the aristocracy lived in castles that towered toward the heavens.

For many centuries, Croats were also divided linguistically; only the peasants and working classes spoke Croatian. Croatian aristocrats identified

These unfinished enclosures show the stages of building a traditional stone house on the Istria Peninsula. The lowly structures protected peasants from the wind.

The Trakošćan Castle near Krapina, Croatia, dates to the thirteenth century but was reconstructed in the nineteenth century to its present appearance by an aristocratic family.

themselves with the upper class of whichever imperial power was ruling Croatia; when Croatia was part of the Austro-Hungarian Empire, most educated Croats spoke and wrote Hungarian or German as their first language. The Illyrian movement that started in the 1830s was supposedly for the revival of the Croatian language; the movement appealed to the Croatian-speaking masses and targeted the upper classes.

In the twentieth century, Croatian and Serbian nationalists came together to take control of parts of Slavonia and Dalmatia under local Serbo-Croatian-speaking governments. Thus, the idea of a united Yugoslavia originated among the masses and was not developed by the country's social and intellectual elites, as it was in many other countries.

COSTUME

The character of Croatia's many regions is reflected in their traditional folk costumes. The most colorful and finely embroidered clothing is found in the rich and fertile Pannonian Plain. In the more rugged Alpine region, both male and female costumes are simpler, often woven from rough, homemade white cloth. On the Dalmatian coast, the traditional dress reflects the mild climate. Today, folk costume is reserved for holidays and special occasions, and people wear typical Western clothing on a day-to-day basis.

Folk costumes and activities were promoted by Tito as a solution to national and ethnic sectarianism, and as an alternative form of social identity and social activity to the church. Following in Tito's footsteps, President Tudjman promoted folk activities and made use of folk motifs. The political attention to elements of folklore in the culture has not only preserved the costumes, traditions, and artifacts of folklore, but has also assisted Croatia in maintaining the spirit of folklore—the harmony of people and their environment.

INTERNET LINKS

https://croatia.eu/article.php?lang=2&id=14
History and statistics about the demographics of the Croatian people, at home and abroad, are provided on this site.

https://www.croatiaweek.com/50-famous-people-with-croatian -heritage
This article showcases fifty celebrities with some Croatian heritage.

https://www.tripsavvy.com/croatian-folk-costumes-1501295
This site presents national costumes from across Croatia.

LIFESTYLE

A young shepherd boy holds a baby goat in a meadow in Djurdjenovac, Croatia.

MANY CROATIANS LIVE RURAL lives, especially when compared to typical lifestyles in many developed countries. Approximately 56.9 percent of Croatians live in urban areas—compared to 82.3 percent urbanization in the United States. Traditions are more evident in the rural village than in the urban city. Social interaction is more clearly formulated and meaningful in rural areas, where people know their neighbors well and meet them every day, than in the city, where strangers pass on the street.

THE LIFE CYCLE

Regardless of religion, all Croatians attach great importance to the main life cycle rites of birth, marriage, and death. All three events must be sanctioned by religious ritual.

The wedding feast is perhaps the most public and expensive rite. A family of modest means will do everything within its power, even going into debt, to provide a memorable wedding. This is particularly true in the countryside, where the entire village may be invited—or two villages if the marriage is between people from different villages. Even in the

7

Smoking, alcohol use, and obesity are major health problems in Croatia and are especially concerning in adolescents. More fifteen-year-olds smoke than in any other EU country, except for Bulgaria. Adolescent alcohol use is also higher, particularly among boys. Obesity rates are rising among children, where the rate grew by 50 percent between 2001 and 2014.

towns, a wedding provides an occasion for distant relatives to come together, and these relatives expect to be invited and to feast.

Weddings involve folk elements as well as church rituals. Today, it is common to have a large church wedding followed by an even larger secular celebration, attended by friends and relatives.

THE FAMILY

Traditionally, the basic social unit in Croatia is the nuclear family—a husband, wife, and three or four children. However, in recent years, the birthrate has declined to 1.4 children per family. In the event of a divorce, Croatian law states that parents are equally responsible for the care of their children. The law also ensures that both partners receive half of all the property and assets.

A widowed grandparent will often share the living quarters and have a close relationship with the children. In rural areas, an extended family living together is more common. Compared with households in the cities, family units in rural areas tend to be larger. In Croatia, it is normal for the elderly to be cared for by their children or grandchildren. In farming communities, this is guaranteed because the land and house are likely to pass from father to son.

Given the economic uncertainties since independence and the fact that retirement pensions are minimal, this arrangement is likely to survive well into the future.

EDUCATION

Education in Croatia has a long history. Records from the tenth century show Tomislav, the first king of Croatia, exhorting his subjects to send their children to school so they might become learned monks and nuns. Several monastic centers of higher education led to the opening of what began as the first known Croatian university, founded in Zagreb by Jesuits in 1669. It mainly taught classical philology, law, philosophy, and theology.

Today, Croatia spends roughly 4.6 percent of its GDP on education, which is below the European average and below the average 5 to 7 percent spent by most developed countries. All education is paid for by the state; however, low pay has led to a chronic shortage of teachers throughout the country.

Education is compulsory for eight years. Elementary education begins at age six or seven and continues through to eighth grade at age fifteen. At that point, children can go on to secondary (high school) education. They normally go to either a vocational school or a gymnasium (specialized academic school) that concentrates on sciences, technology and mathematics, or languages. Literacy is close to 100 percent.

Today, there are eight universities in Croatia's larger cities: Zagreb, Osijek, Rijeka, Zadar, Dubrovnik (where there are two universities), Pula, and Split. The quality of education, especially in science, medicine, and engineering, is on par with the highest international standards. In addition, there are numerous polytechnic schools, business colleges, and other vocational education institutions.

HEALTH

The quality of medical care in Croatia meets international standards, and health care is free to all citizens. Life expectancy is 76.3 years, roughly on par with much of the developed world.

In general, the health situation is favorable. Compared with some other parts of the former Yugoslavia, Croatia has few severely war-injured people to care for. There are no disease epidemics spreading through the population, and even the mosquitoes carry no dangerous diseases and prefer to stay near the lakes and forests. Tick-borne Lyme disease, however, is endemic throughout the country.

Most important, nobody goes hungry. The country has abundant grain, livestock, and seafood, and Croatians who are temporarily down on their luck are likely to be fed by relatives, neighbors, and (such are their norms of hospitality) even by strangers.

However, a larger than average number of Croatians smoke tobacco—roughly 36 percent of the population in 2015 (compared to 17 percent in the United States)—and this has resulted in a high rate of smoking-related diseases.

A tradition of spa healing exists in Croatia and goes back to Roman times, when the building of *thermae* (THER-me) began. Some of the original Roman structures are still in use; other spas are modern resorts. Croatia has numerous mineral water springs, including thermal springs, medicinal mud centers, and a medicinal oil center. Croatians believe that if one goes to the right center, almost any human affliction can be alleviated or cured. The most commonly stated reasons for "taking the waters" are rheumatic diseases, skin problems, inflammation of the muscles, respiratory disorders, and stress. Many older Croatians go regularly to a spa.

THE POSITION OF WOMEN

Women have been equal under the law in educational institutions and in the workplace since Croatia became a member of the former Yugoslavia in 1945. In the twenty-first century, it might be expected that women would have positions of real equality. However, this is not the case. Almost half of the workforce is female, but Croatians tend to rationalize this as a necessity in order for a family to achieve a living wage.

Croatian women typically earn only two-thirds as much as their male counterparts, although slightly more Croatian women go on to higher education than men. Home tasks such as taking care of children, cooking, and cleaning are generally considered to be a woman's natural role. For many women, professional equality has led to a situation where they have modern rights in the workplace and traditional duties at home, leading to a greater burden for women than for men.

Mothers fair relatively well in childbirth, with a 2015 maternal mortality rate of 8 deaths per 100,000 live births. This statistic is typically used to gauge the quality of women's pregnancy- and childbirth-related health care in a given country. Croatia's rate placed it at number 156 out of 184 nations—the higher the number, the lower the mortality rate. For comparison, at number 139, the US maternal mortality rate that year was 14 deaths per 100,000 live births.

INTERNET LINKS

https://croatia.eu/page.php?lang=2&id=18
This site has information about the Croatian lifestyle and educational system.

https://ec.europa.eu/health/sites/health/files/state/docs/chp_hr_english.pdf
This 2017 health profile for Croatia compares statistics across the EU.

https://www.who.int/countries/hrv/en
The World Health Organization provides data and statistics relating to a broad range of health topics in Croatia.

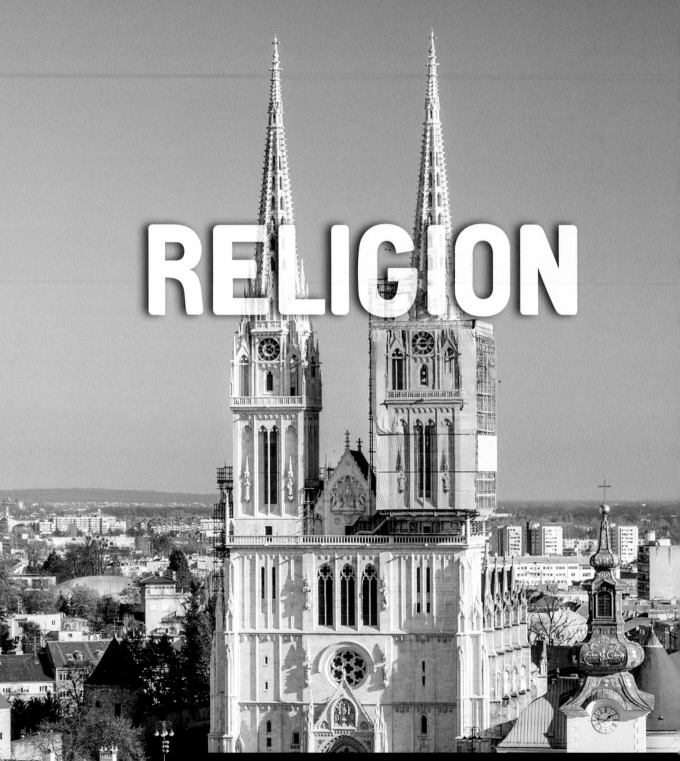

RELIGION

The spires of Zagreb Cathedral dominate this view of Upper Town, a district in Croatia's capital city.

8

ALTHOUGH CROATIA IS OFFICIALLY A secular state, the Roman Catholic religion is very dominant in everyday life. According to the most recent census in 2011, approximately 86.3 percent of Croatians are Roman Catholic, 4.4 percent are Eastern Orthodox Christian, about 1.5 percent are Muslim, 3.8 percent are not religious, and the rest are "others" (including small Jewish and Protestant communities). Most Croatians are Roman Catholics, and almost all Serbs follow the Eastern Orthodox form of Christianity. Freedom of religion is guaranteed by law.

The vast majority of Croatians declare themselves as religious believers. Religion is considered an important part of ethnic identity throughout the Balkans, and even nonreligious Croatians would claim at least minimal membership of the religion of their community. Recent surveys suggest that at least a third of Catholic Croatians attend Mass every week.

Zagreb Cathedral, also called the Cathedral of the Assumption of Mary, is the tallest building in Croatia. Dating from the thirteenth century, with significant reconstruction from 1880 to 1906 following an earthquake, its two spires are visible from most parts of the city.

CATHOLICS

Before arriving in Croatia in the seventh century CE, the Croats were polytheist. Two centuries later, the Croats allied themselves with Roman Catholicism. Today, nearly all Croatians are Roman Catholics. However, for the forty-five years that Croats and Serbs were united in Yugoslavia, the Croats did not parade their Catholicism. There is a historical reason for this. During World War II, the fascist Ustaše regime seized on religious difference and purged the population of Serbs and Jews. Extermination camps and the massacres of Serbs in villages led to revenge killings of Croats in Serbian areas. When Tito came to power, he suppressed religion as an active element of Yugoslav life.

In 1979, however, a large Catholic-Croatian pilgrimage to Rome was held to present a written renewal of Croatian baptismal vows. This pilgrimage celebrated centuries of Catholicism at a time when Catholics in communist Yugoslavia usually maintained a low profile in the face of official attempts to downplay religion and upgrade traditional folklore. Pope John Paul II received the pilgrims and held mass for them in the Croatian language.

When Croatia declared independence, the Vatican was the first state to recognize the republic. Suddenly, churches were full and religious holidays were taken seriously as Croatians outwardly demonstrated their identity as Catholics.

Saint Mark's Roman Catholic Church in Upper Town is another iconic church in Zagreb.

PROTESTANTS

Most Croatians in the small Protestant minority belong to the Lutheran Church or the Reformed Christian Church. The number of Protestants grew in Croatia in the eighteenth century with the migration of Slovaks, Hungarians, and Germans to the area. Some were recruited to the German occupation forces during World War II. As a result, many Protestants faced persecution after the war and fled the country. Today, those who remain enjoy good relations with other faiths.

ISLAM

Islam was present in Croatia even before the invasion of the Muslim Ottoman Empire in the fifteenth and sixteenth centuries. Muslims were living in the eastern part of Croatia as early as the tenth century, and Islamic Ottoman settlements were well established in the twelfth century.

The oldest surviving mosque in the region is in Ustikolina (now a part of Bosnia and Herzegovina); it was constructed fifty years before the Ottomans conquered the town in 1463. The Ottoman Empire did not introduce Islam but raised it to the status of a major religion in the region in the fifteenth century.

The Islamic Center and Mosque opened in 2013 in Rijeka. It was the first mosque in that city and the third in all of Croatia.

ORTHODOXY

Virtually all ethnic Serbs adhere to the Orthodox form of Christianity. Centuries-old doctrinal differences with the Roman Catholic majority are very much alive. The current head of the Serbian Orthodox Church as of 2019 is the patriarch Irinej (b. 1930), who is the spiritual head of all Serbian Orthodox worshippers. Irinej was appointed in 2010 and is the forty-fifth patriarch.

Unlike Roman Catholics, Orthodox Christians allow priests to be married and do not accept the authority of the Pope. The distinctions between Orthodox Christians and Catholics are every bit as deep as those between Catholics and Protestants and have exacerbated conflicts for more than a century between the two groups. Unfortunately, there has been little attempt by religious leaders of either side to overcome their differences, and religious authorities have sometimes supported the conflict.

Among the many places of local pilgrimage for Catholic Croatians, none is as popular or more revered than the village of Medjugorje, which is located inside southern Bosnia and Herzegovina, near the Croatian border. The village is home to four thousand ethnic Croats, all devout Catholics.

On June 24 and 25, 1981, when the region was a part of Yugoslavia, the Virgin Mary reportedly appeared at separate times to six local young people, aged fifteen to sixteen. They claimed that Mary spoke to each, in perfect Croatian, and gave them messages to be passed to the world. The vision is known as Our Lady of Medjugorje. The village is now a popular place for Catholic pilgrims and is home to an important shrine to the Virgin Mary. Millions of people from all over the world have visited the village since the vision appeared.

JUDAISM

The first Jews are recorded to have entered Croatian cities in 723 CE, when the Byzantine Empire expelled them. Communities of Jews settled in Split and Dubrovnik after fleeing persecution in Spain in 1491 and Portugal in 1496. Jews living in Croatia acquired full civil rights and equality in 1873 and participated in all aspects of life in the country, excelling in the arts, sciences, and humanities, and assisting Croatia's attempts to build an education system and a modern economy.

However, the Jewish community of twenty thousand was virtually destroyed during World War II, when Croats under the anti-Semitic Nazi leadership established death camps and conducted massacres of Jews and Orthodox

Serbs. Between 1941 and 1945, over 80 percent of the Jewish population was seized and sent off to extermination camps.

More recently, Jewish Croatian numbers have been reduced by emigration, mostly to Israel and the United States. The 2011 census recorded 509 Jews living in Croatia. They maintain ties with Bosnian Jews to the east and south.

Today, Jewish relations with other religious groups are described as good. Many Jews intermarry with Croatians of other religions, and it is estimated that 80 percent of Zagreb's Jewish population were born of interfaith marriages.

This synagogue is in the town of Križevci, in the Prigorje region of Croatia.

INTERNET LINKS

https://www.state.gov/reports/2017-report-on-international-religious-freedom/croatia
This is the US Department of State report on religious freedom in Croatia.

https://www.worldatlas.com/articles/religious-beliefs-in-croatia.html
This site provides an overview of religion in Croatia.

LANGUAGE

A man reads the morning newspaper in a café in the town of Rovinj.

9

Whereas the two one-letter words in English are both vowels (I, a), Croatian has five one-letter words, and two of them are consonants: *a* ("but," "and"), *u* ("in"), *i* ("and"), *s* ("with," "from"), and *k* ("to").

THE LANGUAGE OF CROATIA reflects the country's position at the crossroads between East and West—that is, the junction of Eastern Europe, the Mediterranean, and Western Europe. It belongs to the South Slavic branch of the Slavic group of languages, a linguistic grouping that also includes Serbian, Bosnian, and Slovene. In the past, Croatian, Serbian, and Bosnian were often referred to by the term Serbo-Croatian, as if they were a single language.

The speakers of any of the three languages have no trouble understanding the other two. In addition, the structure and vocabulary of the three languages are very similar. The Croatian language is today the official language of the Republic of Croatia and one of three official languages of neighboring Bosnia and Herzegovina.

Before the 1990s war, when Croatian and Serbian were taught as foreign languages abroad, they were taught as a single language, Serbo-Croatian. Most universities abroad now use the collective term "Bosnian, Croatian, Serbian," often abbreviated BCS for convenience, to describe the languages they teach.

The similarity between Serbian and Croatian led to the Novi Sad Agreement (1954), which declared the two to be a single language with two variants. In the communist era, the Yugoslavian government sought to minimize differences between the main nationalities of the republic, and smoothing out the differences between Serbian and Croatian become one of a number of ways of doing this. In the 1960s and 1970s, groups of Croatian and Serbian linguists independently rejected the Novi Sad Agreement, each group writing and arguing in a language they termed Croatian or Serbian, depending on which side of the ethnic divide they were on. All arguments were fully understood by the other side without any translation.

The Yugoslav authorities imposed official unity on the languages with a heavy hand, and in the 1980s, they banned and burned a number of scholarly publications maintaining that the Croatian language was a separate entity. With independence in 1991 and the subsequent war between Croatia and Serbia, the political decision that Croatian and Serbian were separate and distinct languages became generally accepted. Croatian is, therefore, a language in its own right in the same way that Croats are a people in their own right, because Croatians agree that it should be so.

HISTORICAL DEVELOPMENT

The language or languages spoken by the Illyrian people were spoken throughout what is now Croatia. The words "Dalmatia," "Bosnia," and "Istria" come from Illyrian. The oldest document where the Croatian language is mentioned by name dates to 1177. Croatian was not, however, the earliest indigenous language in Croatia. Before the arrival of the Croats in the seventh century CE, the people of Dubrovnik and neighboring coastal areas spoke Dalmatian. The use of Dalmatian disappeared in favor of Croatian in the fifteenth century, lingering on into the nineteenth century on the island of Krk.

Three regional dialects are recognized in Croatian: Kajkavian, Chakavian, and Shtokavian. Until the fifteenth century, the Chakavian dialect was dominant in Croatia and a large part of Bosnia. From the seventeenth century, the Shtokavian dialect was more widely used, and over the following century it became accepted as standard Croatian.

THE WRITTEN LANGUAGE

Modern Croatian is referred to as *Hrvatski književni jezik,* or just *Hrvatski.* Croatian uses the Latin alphabet, like English and other Western European languages.

The beginning of the Croatian written language can be traced to the ninth century, when Old Church Slavonic was adopted as the language of the liturgy by the clergy. The oldest writing style in the area, known as the Glagolitic script (a type of Slavic script), supposedly dates from around this time, although experts have struggled to trace the origins of the script. Many scholars believe the script was the invention of a Greek missionary named Cyril, who traveled the area converting people to Christianity in the eleventh century. The argument for Cyril seems likely, as he would have known the Slavic language and would have used it when preaching. It appears that Cyril single-handedly constructed a script based on early Greek writing for this purpose.

The earliest known example of Glagolitic script is an eleventh-century inscription found on Krk Island. What happened to Cyril is a mystery, but ecclesiastical, or religious, works in Glagolitic continued to appear for the next two centuries.

Also in use was the Cyrillic script, originating from Greek and refined during the invention of the Russian script. Cyrillic was in use in Dubrovnik, parts of the Dalmatian coast, and Bosnia and Herzegovina. It fell out of use in the nineteenth century when the universal European Latin alphabet took over. Cyrillic remains the preferred script of Serbia (it is also used in other Eastern European languages, in particular Russian). Thus, the written forms of the Croatian and Serbian languages serve as national symbols dividing Croatia and Serbia.

THE SPOKEN LANGUAGE

Modern Croatian is spoken by some 4.5 million people (97 percent of the population) within Croatia and by at least another million Croatians living in other states of the former Yugoslavia, especially in Bosnia and Herzegovina.

It is also spoken, to varying degrees of fluency, by an unknown proportion of up to 2.5 million ethnic Croatians living overseas.

Unlike in English, every letter is pronounced in Croatian, and a letter's sound does not change from one word to another. When a syllable is stressed, it may have either a rising or a falling tone. As for which syllable of a word is stressed, the general rule is that the last syllable is never emphasized; usually, the first syllable is accented.

Serbian is spoken by the Serb minority, although generally as a second language and only when speaking to other Serb speakers. Bosnian, Hungarian, and Slovenian are also spoken by small numbers of minority peoples.

GREETINGS

Greetings are much the same throughout the countries of the former Yugoslavia. Shaking hands is universally acceptable. Touching people of the same sex is more frequent than in Western Europe or the United States; hands on shoulders and knees are tolerated. Kissing on both cheeks is more often seen between women, but kissing between men is not rare. Good friends may sometimes kiss on the mouth, as is common in Russia.

Croatian Muslims usually conform to the basic spoken pattern of *zdravo* (ZDRAH-vo), which means "hello," and *dovidjenja* (do-vee-JEN-yah), meaning "good-bye." Most are tolerant of Western European customs. Among themselves, however, Muslims will sometimes replace Croatian greetings with Arabic greetings typical in Islamic communities.

THE MEDIA

Freedom of speech is granted in Article 38 of the Constitution of the Republic of Croatia, which states: "Freedom of thought and expression are guaranteed. Freedom of thought especially refers to freedom of the press and other media, freedom of speech and public appearance and founding of all the media. Censorship is forbidden by law. Journalists are entitled to free reporting and unlimited access to information. A person whose constitutional rights are violated by public information is entitled to seek redress."

In practice, however, freedom of the press isn't quite that free. Journalists who investigate corruption tend to be harassed—sometimes physically—and are increasingly subject to lawsuits. Defamation is criminalized, and insulting "the Republic, its emblem, its national hymn or flag" is punishable by up to three years in prison. Media content deemed to be "humiliating" has been outlawed since 2013, even if the news is true. In spring 2019, several hundred Croatian journalists rallied in Zagreb to protest the curbing of media freedoms and the use of lawsuits to stop reporting. There were more than 1,100 lawsuits filed against journalists in the country at that point.

THE INTERNET   Like most places in the world, Croatians can get all their international news, entertainment, and other services via the internet. There is a noncommercial site with Croatian news in English—the Croatian Information Centre, http://www.hic.hr/english—as well as a government-owned news site, Hina, https://www.hina.hr/english. Other English-language news sites include Total Croatia News, https://www.total-croatia-news.com and CroatiaWeek, https://www.croatiaweek.com. The *Dubrovnik Times* also publishes online in English at https://www.thedubrovniktimes.com/news/croatia. About 72.7 percent of all Croatians are linked to the internet.

INTERNET LINKS

https://www.omniglot.com/writing/croatian.htm
Omniglot provides a good introduction to the Croatian language.

https://rsf.org/en/croatia
Reporters Without Borders reports annually on the state of press freedom in each country.

ARTS

SPLITSKA BANKA

Split, the second-largest city in Croatia, is full of concrete, Yugoslav-style architecture from the 1970s.

10

C ROATIAN ART, LIKE HUMAN LIFE itself, can be traced back thousands of years. Today, a continuous link with the past influences the modern art and enriches the cultural life of Croatia. Throughout the ages, folk art and crafts have also survived and are celebrated.

MUSIC

Musical texts in neumatic notation date from the eleventh century, and in 1177, the Vatican made note of people "singing in their Croatian language."

For the next three centuries, Croatian music followed the same path of development as in the rest of Europe. One notable exception is Gregorian hymns and chants, which are performed today much as they were in fourteenth-century Croatia.

Although it is known that many dramas of the fifteenth and sixteenth centuries included songs and music, usually of the folk variety, few have survived in written form. Secular Croatian music developed during the eighteenth and nineteenth centuries. This was in part because of the influence from Germany, and in part because of a growing movement to base music on Croatian tradition. There are many Croatian composer-musicians from this period and beyond: Elena Pucić-Sorkočević (1786—1865), the first known female Croatian composer; Ivan Zajc (1832—1914), a student of the Italian opera composer Giuseppe Verdi, who composed more than one thousand pieces of music, many of which

Croatia is home to an amazingly wide range of architectural styles. Ancient Roman ruins in Split, Pula, and elsewhere contrast with glassy, steel, and white-walled modernist structures in Zagreb and beyond. In between, there are the fortified medieval towns of Dubrovnik and Korčula and masterpieces of Romanesque, Renaissance, and Baroque architectural styles evident in churches and public buildings.

A crowd cheers at an electronic music festival in the Roman amphitheater in Pula.

remain popular today; and Vilko Novak (1909—2003), a nationalist composer who wrote "Croatia, God and the Croats" and "Hail to the Homeland."

Pop music is very popular among young Croatians today. Croatia's homegrown pop music resembles the canzone music of Italy, but with an element of traditional music. Croatian pop music is played at one of the many local music festivals each year. The annual Split festival often produces the best summer hits. There are also many Croatian rock bands that are known mainly in Croatia.

THE PERFORMING ARTS

Croatian drama has long ties to the main European theatrical traditions. Dramas of French origin were performed in Zagreb for the public on religious holidays in the twelfth century. These early plays were based on Bible stories, the life of Christ, or legends of the saints. In spite of the religious motifs and the use of Latin by the actors, these plays contained a realistic description of everyday life.

Religion and realism continued to be linked in the thirteenth to the fifteenth centuries. One can learn a lot about pastoral life in the past from the plays of that time, when Croatian drama was said to have come of age. Famous Croatian playwrights during the Renaissance were Mavro Vetranović (1482—1576), who wrote the first Croatian secular drama, *Diana*; Marko Marulić (1450—1524), who wrote *Judita*, the first drama to be produced in Croatian; and Marin Držić (1508—1567), who was probably the first Croat to have his work translated into other languages.

In the seventeenth century, political commentary entered the world of drama in Ivan Gundulić's (1589—1638) epic poem *Osman*, which celebrated a 1621 victory over the Ottomans by the Poles. The parallel world of despised

The *Well of Life* sculpture graces the entrance to the Croatian National Theater in Zagreb.

Gale Over the Ditch is a 1976 painting by Mijo Kovačić. His work has an enchanted, naïve quality and often depicts peasant life in Croatia.

Ottoman rule and Croatian resistance was clear to every Croat who heard Gundulić's powerful words.

By the nineteenth century, many theaters in Croatia had resident professional companies. Today, watching plays in theaters has become a regular part of life for many Croatians.

PAINTING

The earliest preserved Croatian paintings, from the eleventh century, are religious frescoes in the Romanesque style. In accordance with the medieval tradition, many of the artists did not sign their work. In the late fourteenth and early fifteenth centuries, Renaissance painters put their names on their masterpieces.

The mid-fifteenth century to early sixteenth century is considered the best period for frescoes in Croatia, not only for their artistic merits but also because they depicted life in natural settings. The best-known wall painting from this period is the *Danse Macabre* ("dance of death") fresco. It was completed in 1474 by Master Vincent of Kastav and decorates the church of Saint Mary in Škriljine, Istria. Until the end of the sixteenth century, many of Croatia's artists confined themselves to the illumination of religious texts, filling these books with scenes from both the Bible and history.

Zagreb became an important artistic center during the seventeenth century and remains so today. The eighteenth to nineteenth centuries produced attempts to blend Western European artistic achievements with the Croatian painting tradition. The most famous master of the Zagreb school was Vlaho Bukovac (1855–1922), who painted *The Croatian National Revival* on the curtain of Zagreb's Croatian National Theater.

The twentieth century saw the *Monument to Peace* by Antun Augustinčić (1900–1979) erected outside the United Nations building in New York City. Meanwhile, the artistic world embraced the naïve art of Croatian peasant painters such as Mijo Kovačić (b. 1935), who produced art pieces that many people find meaningful.

Probably the greatest writer of twentieth-century Croatian literature was Miroslav Krleža (1893–1981). Born in Zagreb when Croatia was a part of the crumbling Austro-Hungarian Empire, Krleža studied at a military academy in Budapest and was drafted into the Austrian army during World War I. After surviving the horrors of the war, Krleža established himself as one of a new breed of modernist writers in the newly independent Yugoslavia.

In 1950, Krleža founded the Yugoslav Institute for Lexicography, now called Miroslav Krleža Lexicographical Institute, heading the institute until his death in 1981.

Since his death, critics have revisited his work, and he is generally considered one of the finest European modernist authors of his era, with an original voice, style, and technique. Krleža's collected works number more than fifty volumes and include poetry, dramas, short stories, novels, essays, diaries, and autobiographical work, spanning seven decades. Krleža was a man of ideas who reflected on Yugoslav life, politics, and history. He was particularly interested in humanism and the freedom of the individual mind versus the restrictions of society.

A bronze monument of Miroslav Krleža by Marija Ujević-Galetović stands outside his home in Zagreb.

LITERATURE

The Croatian language was used for inscriptions and religious writings as early as the eleventh century. Literature in Croatia, however, really got going only with the invention of the printing press in the fifteenth century.

Croatian writing of the fifteenth century falls into two categories. One stream continued and expanded the clerical tradition, telling the legends of

Just as the UNESCO World Heritage Center maintains a list of international landmarks and regions considered of outstanding human value, it also tracks international folkways. The name "intangible cultural heritage of humanity" is an umbrella term that includes traditions or living expressions passed on from one generation to another in a particular place. Some examples are "oral traditions, performing arts, social practices, rituals, festive events, knowledge and practices concerning nature and the universe or the knowledge and skills to produce traditional crafts."

As globalization creates a greater sense of international connectedness, it also threatens the unique cultural expressions of small communities. Those folkways that are on the verge of dying out are listed as being "in urgent need of safeguarding."

Croatia has fourteen cultural elements inscribed in the UNESCO List of Intangible Cultural Heritage (ICH); and is included on several other elements that are shared across multiple nations.

- *lacemaking*
- *two-part singing and playing in the Istrian scale*
- *Festival of Saint Blaise, the patron saint of Dubrovnik*
- *annual spring procession of the* kraljice *or* ljelje *("queens") from Gorjani*
- *annual Carnival procession of the Kastav bellringers*
- *Za Križen procession ("following the cross") on the island of Hvar*
- *traditional manufacturing of children's wooden toys in the region of Croatian Zagorje*
- sinjska alka, *a knights' tournament in Sinj*
- *gingerbread craft of northern Croatia*
- bećarac *singing and playing from Slavonia, Baranja and Srijem*
- nijemo kolo *("silent reel"), a silent circle dance of the Dalmatian hinterland*
- klapa *multipart singing of Dalmatia*
- međimurska popevka, *a folksong from the Međimurje region in the northwestern part of Croatia*
- ojkanje *two-part singing of the Dalmatian hinterland, which is inscribed on the list as being "in need of urgent safeguarding"*

the many saints. The other was the humanist tradition, from which developed such works as *Judita* by Marko Marulić (1450—1524)—the first literary work written in the Croatian language by a Croat for a Croatian audience.

In the sixteenth century, Croatian literature was influenced by Italy, and many poems of love, romance, and humor were written. The nineteenth-century Illyrian (National Revival) movement, which greatly influenced the work of artists, was strongly felt by Croatia's writers. This age of Romanticism gave birth to August Šenoa (1838—1881), a prolific writer of historical novels.

In the twentieth century, novelist and playwright Miroslav Krleža became known abroad for two famous novels, *The Return of Philip Latinovicz* (1932) and the multivolume saga *Banners* (1963—1965). Krleža was active in the campaign to achieve equality between the Croatian and Serbian literary languages, and in 1967, he opposed Tito.

Customers search through an outdoor book market in Zagreb.

A small 4-inch (10-cm) circle of fine Pag lace takes a skilled woman artisan up to twenty-five hours of work to produce. The craft probably began as a way to decorate the white linen folk costumes of the island. In the early twentieth century, Pag lace became popular with Austrian nobility and gained a reputation throughout Europe.

Lace-makers pass down the characteristic geometric designs through the family, adding perhaps a small personal touch that can identify an individual or a family. Pag lace is worked without drawings and considered to be among the most delicate and durable in the world. In 2009, Croatian lacemaking, including Hvar lace and Lepoglava lace, along with the Pag style, was added to the UNESCO Representative List of the Intangible Heritage of Humanity.

FILM

In 1896, the first permits for the public showing of films were issued in Croatia. By 1907, permanent movie theaters existed in Zagreb, Split, Rijeka, Sisak, and Zadar. After this enthusiastic start, however, the Croatian film industry ground to a halt. This was due to the adverse economic conditions in Croatia at the beginning of the twentieth century. The film industry got going again only when a need arose for film reports of military action in the 1912 Balkan Wars.

In 1917, the Croatia Film Company (which became the Yugoslavia Film Company in 1918) established in Zagreb one of the first schools for the study of film technique. However, it was not until 1933 that a Croatian director, Oktavijan Miletić, received an international cinematic award, and only after 1953 did Croatia's film industry become internationally known and acclaimed for its animated cartoons.

Outside of the cartoon genre, Croatian cinema has yet to find its place in the global scene, with most movies today being made in the Croatian language and rarely being shown outside of Croatia except at international film festivals.

FOLK ART

Historically, the various Croatian regions were divided into separate political units and tended to come under different cultural and religious influences. The physical division into Pannonian (farmers), Alpine (herders), and Adriatic (fishers, seafarers) also meant that different folk costumes, songs, music, stories, and customs were developed from region to region. Today, these different identities continue to exist within a greater Croatian national identity.

The relative isolation of Croatia's many islands meant that culture and art there developed quite separately from the mainland. On Pag Island, an intricate style of woven lace has been developed over many centuries, while special lavender products were produced on Hvar Island and stone crafts on Brač Island. Similarly, each area will have its interpretation of a dance or song, even if these have crossed original "folk" boundaries to achieve regional or national status.

Little wooden dolls dressed in lavender dresses are for sale in Split.

The tamburica, or tamburitza, is Croatia's national instrument and is used in much of its folk music. It's a small, long-necked string instrument in the lute family. The instrument is thought to have come to the Balkan region from Turkey many centuries ago, and it became popular as an expression of Croatian culture in the nineteenth century. Today, there are many similar instruments with different names throughout Southern and Central Europe.

Tamburicas are held and plucked like guitars but sound like mandolins. Some have body types like lutes (pear-shaped), while others look like little guitars. Within the tambura family of related instruments, the sizes range from very small, like a ukelele, to very large, like a bass viol. They are often played in groups called tamburica orchestras. The smaller the instrument, the higher its pitch, and therefore the largest ones, with longer strings, play the lowest notes.

FOLK MUSIC AND DANCE

Traditional Croatian music is as rich and varied as the country's folk art. The traditional string instruments of the north are accompanied by guitars and accordions on the Dalmatian coast, producing an Italian sound that reflects Italy's influence on this region. Everywhere throughout Croatia the sound of the traditional tamburica—a three- or five-string pear-shaped lute—can be heard. The tamburica is the national instrument of Croatia.

Kolo is a type of dance found throughout Croatia and is probably the nearest thing to a shared folk tradition in the country. The word *kolo* means "circle" or "wheel." The dance is marked by a large circle of men and women who move, usually in a clockwise direction, to the sound of traditional string instruments and local songs. Although all dancers wear folk dress during a kolo, the style varies from place to place.

INTERNET LINKS

https://croatia.eu/page.php?lang=2&id=17
A wide range of Croatian cultural topics are presented on this site.

http://www.croatianhistory.net/etf/art.html
This site provides a very thorough overview of Croatian art.

https://www.croatiatraveller.com/Heritage_Sites/Intangible -Heritage.html
Videos demonstrate Croatia's traditional styles of folk singing, dancing, and crafts found on UNESCO's Intangible Cultural Heritage List.

http://www.mijokovacic.com/en
The Mijo Kovačić Foundation presents a gallery of the artist's paintings.

LEISURE

A boy jumps from a cliff into the Adriatic Sea.

11

C ROATIA HAS BEEN A POPULAR tourist destination since the 1980s, with the islands and coastal resorts of Split and Dubrovnik proving attractive destinations for tourists who enjoy rich heritage with plenty of sunshine in a laid-back atmosphere.

Tourism declined rapidly in the 1990s, with the War of Independence and the ethnic strife in the region, but into the new century, tourist numbers are back up to their prewar levels.

Croatians have at their fingertips almost the full range of leisure activities. Some of these include listening to classical, modern, and folk music; dancing in early-morning jazz clubs or dance clubs (also called discos); having a simple meal at an inn or feasting in a top-class restaurant; hunting in a virgin forest; skiing in a resort overlooking the blue Adriatic Sea; mountaineering; and water sports.

Whether they are participating or simply watching, being active or just sitting with a drink in the town square, Croatians are never at a loss for ways to relax and enjoy life after a hard day's work.

CULTURAL ACTIVITIES

For forty-five years, the communist government subsidized opera, concerts, theaters, museums, and many other cultural activities to make them available to everyone. As a result of this legacy, winter evenings in Croatia are warmed by the opportunity to attend national and international art events at prices that remain among the lowest in Europe.

Some of the beaches along the Adriatic Coast are pebbled rather than sandy, but that doesn't prevent locals and tourists alike from enjoying a wide range of water-related activities. The scenery is often spectacular and the seawater, is clear and clean.

In warm weather, Croatians can express their love for culture at summer festivals that take place in many towns. Shakespeare's play *Twelfth Night* takes on a special significance when it is performed in the ancient Lovrijenac fortress in Dubrovnik—Shakespeare's setting for *Twelfth Night* is "a city in Illyria." In Pula, the beauty of a music recital in what is the world's third-largest and arguably Europe's best-preserved Roman amphitheater is guaranteed to move any audience.

Such spectacular events were established long before tourism became significant. Today, they attract international performers and an international audience.

TRADITIONAL GAMES

There are a few traditional sports or games unique to Croatia. One is *balote* (BA-lo-te), a bowling game that was developed in Dalmatia.

Another is *alka* (AHL-kah). Croatians call this a game, but it has been likened to a battle. Held in August, alka involves a freely interpreted reconstruction of the defeat of the Ottomans in 1715 at the hands of the outnumbered Croats of Sinj. Men on horses will try to push their lances through a row of rings hanging from a rope, all the while galloping at breakneck speed. The games provide an occasion for the *alkali* (AHL-kah-lee), the renowned horsemen of Sinj, to dress up and demonstrate their horsemanship.

SPORTS

The earliest known written account of a sport in Croatia appeared in 1767 and referred to a series of fishing boat races between the port cities of Split and Makarska.

Zagreb has long been the center of organized sports in Croatia. The popularity of hunting and the seeming inevitability of military conflict perhaps gave rise to the Marksmen's Society, the first sporting organization, established in 1786. This was followed after some time by a number of European-oriented sporting institutions, such as the Gymnastics Club (1874) and the Mountaineering Society (1875).

Football (soccer) is the country's most popular national spectator sport, with Croatia doing well against more established, better financed, and more famous clubs in the European championships. In the 2018 FIFA World Cup, Croatia came in second in the competition, achieving its best-ever result, losing only to France in the final. In 2019, Croatia was ranked fifth in the world.

Like most European nations, Croatia has its own sports hall of fame, including Olympic medal winners and recipients of other international awards. These cover a full range of sports, but Croatia excels at ball games such as basketball, water polo, tennis, and handball. Krešimir Ćosić (1948—1995) became the third international player ever elected to the Basketball Hall of Fame in Massachusetts. Dražen Petrović was another extraordinary basketball player who carried the Croatian flag in the international arena, playing in the United States for the New Jersey Nets. His monument stands in Olympic Park in Lausanne, Switzerland. The Croatian national basketball team came in second in the 1992 Olympics, and third in the 1993 and 1995 European Championships.

Kids play soccer on a field at the Kamerlengo Castle, a fifteenth-century fortress in Trogir.

Children and adults enjoy sledding on Medvednica Mountain in December.

Janica Kostelić, born in Zagreb during the Yugoslavia years, is the most successful female alpine ski racer in the history of the Olympic Games, having won four medals—three gold and one silver—at the 2002 Winter Games at Salt Lake City. In 2006, at the Turin Olympics, she won another gold and another silver. After that, she retired due to chronic back and knee pain. Since 2016, she has been the state secretary for science, education, and sports in the Croatian government.

In tennis, Mirjana Lučić won the 1998 Australian Open Women's Doubles at the age of fifteen, while ranked outsider Goran Ivanišević won the Wimbledon Men's Singles title in 2001. More recently, the Croatian Davis Cup team won the 2005 Davis Cup—the World Cup of tennis—while the team reached the semifinal in 2009, led by their best player of recent years, Marin Cilić. In 2018, Croatia won the Davis Cup a second time, led again by Cilić as well as by

Borna Corić. That year, Croatia was the only nation with two tennis players in the world's top fifteen—both Cilić and Corić.

The Croatian men's national handball team became Olympic champions twice, in 1996 and 2004, and also won the gold medal at the 2003 World Men's Handball Championship and the silver medal in 2005 and 2009. The team won a bronze at the 2012 Olympic Games in London.

SAILING AND DIVING

Sailing and diving are very popular with both Croatians and foreigners. Croatia has more than forty marinas, fully equipped with services, shops, and restaurants. Several marinas run sailing schools that are popular with Croatians, many of whom own some sort of seagoing vessel.

A growing number of Croatians are joining foreign tourists in sailing and diving off Croatia's long coastline and around the hundreds of islands of the Adriatic. Numerous diving schools exist, and Croatia provides the clearest, safest, and nearest sea for Europeans interested in learning the sport or simply experiencing the underwater world of colorful fish and corals.

HUNTING

Croatians enjoy a long tradition of hunting for both food and sport. It is possible to retain this aspect of national culture because of the favorable ratio of population to land resources. Croatia contains virgin forest land that is rare in other European countries. Some 38.2 percent of Croatia is forested, and hundreds of areas have been set aside for hunting. Twenty-five thousand licenses are allocated annually for the hunting of big game (deer, wild boar, and bear) and 320,000 for small game (mouflon, pheasant, partridge, and hare).

In recent years, there have been signs that business interests are putting pressure on the timber and furniture export industries to expand, leading to rapid deforestation. Also, even the most progressive system of forest reserves can do little against the destructive effects of acid rain creeping down from Croatia's industrialized northern neighbors.

Two women immerse themselves in a muddy bath at one of Croatia's many thermal spas.

HEALTH SPAS

Around Zagreb and on the coast, there are numerous health spas at local mineral springs. Croatians advancing in years, sportsmen relaxing their muscles, and anybody seeking a cure for or relief from a variety of health problems can be found in Croatia's many thermal springs. Many young Croatians also follow the tradition of their parents and ancestors and regularly drink the waters or relax in them. All will testify that the Croatians' good standard of health owes much to their spa habit.

NIGHTLIFE

For locals and tourists alike, there are nightclubs and casinos, as well as folk and jazz clubs. Many such spots remain open until 4:00 a.m.

An alternative activity is the *kino* (KEE-no), the low-priced and very popular cinema, where Croatians watch mostly foreign films with their original soundtrack. A kino may show several different movies in one evening, starting with family entertainment and moving on to more adult themes later in the evening and past midnight.

On summer nights, many Croatians prefer to remain outdoors, taking a stroll on the town piazza and enjoying one of the many open-air restaurants.

SHOPPING

Two of the mysteries of modern Croatian life are how a struggling economy manages to stock such a wide variety of shops with mostly imported clothing and how people with little spare money purchase these stylish outfits to wear to the office or for an evening of leisure.

The economic difficulties that followed the war and Croatia's independence have not stopped Croatians from shopping; quite the opposite. Croatians spend more time in the shops than they ever did, buying the latest fashions and electronic goods. If shopping is now more expensive, Croatians cut down on their trips to the fashion houses of neighboring Italy and are even more determined to get value for their money—and to enjoy doing so.

INTERNET LINKS

https://croatia.eu/article.php?lang=2&id=51
Popular sports in Croatia are covered on this site, with many links to related information.

https://hns-cff.hr/en
The homepage of Croatia's Football (soccer) Federation delivers the news in English.

FESTIVALS

A dapper accordion player pleases the crowd at the Rijeka Carnival celebration in 2019.

12

W ITH A MOSTLY CATHOLIC population, Croatia celebrates the most important Christian holidays as national holidays. That means everyone gets the day off, regardless of their religion or heritage. People of other faiths are free to observe their own religious holy days as well, but those are more private affairs.

For Christians, not only are the essential days of Christmas and Easter celebrated, but also some fests which are particularly Catholic holidays, such as the Assumption. For the faithful, August 15 marks the day when the Virgin Mary ascended into heaven. Other religious holy days observed as national holidays are Epiphany, January 6; Corpus Christi (Body of Christ) Day in late spring; All Saints' Day, November 1; and Saint Stephen's Day, December 26.

The remaining national holidays are state-oriented, including observances of independence and other historical dates of importance.

RELIGIOUS HOLIDAYS

Since Croatia's independence, many religious traditions have been revived. For example, more Croatians now commemorate Lent, which observes the forty days leading up to Easter as a time of somber contemplation and personal sacrifice.

Just before the solemn Lenten season begins, people enjoy raucous festivities called Carnival. Every year, the celebrations feature elaborate

For Croatian children, Christmas starts on December 5, the eve of Saint Nicholas Day. That night, they leave their shoes on a windowsill for good Saint Nick to fill. In the morning, they will find their shoes filled with sweets and little toys, but naughty kids might find twigs left by the bogeyman Krampus, who threatens to beat disobedient children with branches.

Traditional parade musicians dressed in colorful costumes play in the 2019 Carnival procession in Matulji.

and spectacular processions that attract visitors from within and outside Croatia. Each town has its own Carnival. Perhaps the most elaborate and longest are those held in Samobor, a town known for its folk traditions and crafts, and Rijeka, where businesses close and the entire town gives itself up to seven days of celebrations every year. Carnivals are colorful and exciting, featuring parades of richly decorated floats, marvelously costumed marchers, musicians, and dancers; puppet shows; theatrical performances; and more.

Each Carnival has its own local flavor as well. In Rijeka, this is apt to include a procession of Zvončari (bell ringers) from the nearby town of Kastav. Dressed in sheepskins and animal masks, they roam the streets to welcome the spring and drive out evil spirits. The Zvončari wear white slacks, blue and white T-shirts, a sheepskin, a red bandana, and, of course, bells. Since 2009, this tradition has been included on the UNESCO list of Intangible Cultural Heritage.

Holy Week, which leads up to Easter Sunday, is another occasion when neighbors and townspeople gather together for festivities. For the faithful, the week commemorates the final days in the life of Jesus, leading to his crucifixion on Good Friday and his resurrection on Easter Sunday. On the islands of Brač, Hvar, and Korčula, people participate in religious processions. In central Croatia, people light bonfires to mark Holy Week.

Christmas is the high point of the year. Bright lights and decorations illuminate town squares and marketplaces. Croatians gather with their extended family to celebrate with joy and feasting. Faithful Catholics also attend packed church services, especially midnight Mass, after a traditional Christmas Eve dinner of *baklar* (a cod stew), with *fritule* (fried sugared donuts) for dessert. On Christmas day, the family will gather around the Christmas tree, give gifts, and then enjoy a big feast. The following day, called Saint Stephen's Day, is for visiting relatives. The Croatian identity is reinforced through these traditional celebrations.

TRADITIONAL FESTIVALS

The origins of some popular traditional festivals have been lost over time, like the crossbow competition held on Rab Island in July. There, men in colorful Renaissance clothing compete to shoot arrows at targets.

Some traditions date back centuries. The three-day Alka Festival (also known as the Tilters Tournament) takes place in the tiny town of Sinj every August. The event dates to 1715, when seven hundred Croats defeated sixty thousand Ottoman soldiers at the Battle of Sinj. Events include jousting and a competition between Sinj horsemen to spear hanging rings with the tip of a lance while riding at full gallop.

Other festivals date back even farther in history. The Days of Diocletian, a summer-long festival that takes place in the city of Split, relives the days when the Roman emperor Diocletian walked the city around 300 CE. Today, Roman legions line the city streets when "Emperor Diocletian" rides by during a parade in his honor. Street performers entertain the crowds, and the streets ring with the sounds of fanfares, drums, and music. All of the fun takes place around the ruins of Diocletian's ancient palace in the Old Town.

The following occasions are national holidays for all Croatians. Typically, government offices, banks, and schools close, and most people have the day off.

New Year's Day . . . . *January 1*
Epiphany . . . . *January 6*
Easter Monday . . . . *March/April*
Labor Day . . . . *May 1*
Corpus Christi Day . . . . *May/June*
Antifascist Resistance Day . . . . . *June 22*
National Day . . . . *June 25*
Homeland Thanksgiving Day . . . . *August 5*
Assumption of Mary . . . . *August 15*
Independence Day . . . . *October 8*
All Saints' Day . . . . *November 1*
Christmas Day . . . . *December 25*
Saint Stephen's Day . . . . *December 26*

ARTS AND SUMMER FESTS

Croatia has many arts festivals, and most occur in the summer. These galas attract both tourists and locals to enjoy the fun and the warm summer nights.

The most prestigious event in all of Croatia is the Dubrovnik Summer Festival, which started in 1950. Taking place from mid-July to mid-August, this festival showcases theater, concerts, and dance in several open-air locations around the city. Besides Dubrovnik, Zagreb, Split, and Osor (a town on Cres Island) also have their own summer festivals.

Also in July and August, the Zadar Summer of Theater showcases local and international stage, dance, and music performances. The festival was first held in 1995 and has become one of Croatia's more important summer festivals. There is also a world-famous film festival, Motovun Film Festival, held in Motovun, Istria. It usually takes place over five to six days in late July or early August.

In the city of Šibenik, there is a festival just for children. The International Children's Festival starts in the last week of June or in the first week of July. There are workshops in crafts, music, dance, children's film, and theater.

In Zagreb, there is a movie festival that takes place every October, and the beautiful coastal town of Split hosts an International Festival of New Film annually. A Festival of Art is held in Rovinj, where painters get the opportunity to display their work.

INTERNET LINKS

**https://croatia.hr/en-GB/Activities-and-attractions/Events/
NewEvents/dubrovnik-summer-festival-0**
Photos and information about the Dubrovnik Summer Festival are found on this tourism site.

**https://www.croatiaweek.com/christmas-croatian-style-15-foods
-you-will-find-on-the-table**
Bright photos of traditional Croatian Christmas foods are presented on this site.

**https://ich.unesco.org/en/RL/annual-carnival-bell-ringers-pageant
-from-the-kastav-area-00243**
The bell ringers of Kastav are an example of "Intangible Cultural Heritage of Humanity," as described on this site.

https://ich.unesco.org/en/state/croatia-HR
This is the UNESCO Intangible Cultural Heritage page for Croatia.

https://www.timeanddate.com/holidays/croatia
This calendar site for national holidays and other events updates yearly.

The popular and colorful Dubrovnik Farmers Market in the historical Old Town features outdoor stalls of locally grown, fresh produce.

13

FROM THE TRUFFLES OF ISTRIA—THE underground fungi kind, not the chocolates—to the sausages of Slavonia, Croatian cuisine is a kaleidoscope of regional variety.

The Dalmatian coast enjoys a Mediterranean climate and a Mediterranean diet that consists mainly of seafood, boiled or grilled on open fires and seasoned with olive oil and herbs. The food is often served with rice and washed down with strong red wine. On the other hand, the continental north, which experiences cold winters, serves up hearty meat dishes, accompanied by potatoes and a light wine.

FOREIGN INFLUENCE

Italy, just across the Adriatic Sea from Dalmatia, has strongly influenced the food of the coastal region, and pizza, spaghetti, and risotto are popular. A typical meal would begin with thin slivers of smoked ham as an appetizer, followed by *prstaci* (prer-STAH-tsee), a pasta topped with seafood, or *brodet* (BRO-det), a mixed fish stew with rice.

The tastes of Hungary, Austria, and Turkey are readily discernible in the north and east. Croatians in the Zagreb region expect plenty of meat on their plates. Pork, lamb, turkey, and duck are roasted, very often on a spit in the traditional fashion. Veal steaks are stuffed with ham and cheese and fried in breadcrumbs.

A typical inland meal is not light on calories. Even in modest households, the main meal of the day, eaten either at noon or in the evening, may begin with baked cheese dumplings called *strukli* (SHTROO-klee) or a simple potato soup. This may be followed by *gulas* (GOO-lahsh), or goulash,

Croatians generally eat two heavy meals a day. They usually skip breakfast, but if they don't, it is likely to be a cold slice of rich *burek* and a strongly brewed espresso coffee served in a tiny cup.

Kulen, the Croatian spicy sausage, is served on a wooden board.

as much a staple in this part of Croatia as it is in Hungary, and finished off with *palaćinka* (PAH-lah-cheen-kah), pancakes filled with jam and topped with chocolate.

The eastern Slavonia region is known for its liberal use of paprika and garlic. Here the meat diet is varied with river fish, mostly carp and pike, traditionally steamed in paprika sauce and served with noodles. *Kulen* (KOO-len), a paprika-flavored sausage, is eaten as a snack or served with cottage cheese, peppers, pickled vegetables, and chunks of bread as an evening meal. Cakes stuffed with walnuts, poppy seeds, and plum jam often mark the end of a meal.

REGIONAL SPECIALITIES

Croatia is one of the few countries in Europe that continues to enjoy fresh game from under-exploited forests; fresh fish from large territorial salt waters,

Though Croatians have hunted truffles for centuries, the country is still not known for the prized underground fungi in the same way that France and Italy are. However, that could soon change.

Truffles are said by the Croatians to be the most delicious mushrooms in the world and are surrounded with a mystical folklore. They are not cultivated but are found wild in the forests, most abundantly in the Istria region.

Croatians have bred and trained special truffle-hunting dogs called breks *(BREKS) to sniff out the prized mushrooms during the three-month truffle season from October to January. France, Italy, and Spain are the traditional truffle producers and consumers, but Croatian truffles are said to be*

tastier and cost half the price of those sold by their more experienced counterparts. A typical cherry-sized truffle can sell for as much as $30, and the white truffle—a delicacy—can sell for as much as $7,000 per 2.2 pounds (1 kilogram)—or more! One of the largest reported truffles in the world was found in 1999 by Giancarlo Zigante and his dog, Diana, near Buje, in Istria. The truffle weighed 2 pounds, 14 ounces (1.3 kilograms).

Each September, the town of Buzet in Istria, the self-proclaimed "City of Truffles," hosts a truffle festival. The festivities include the cooking of a giant dish of scrambled eggs, using more than two thousand eggs and 22 pounds (10 kg) of truffles.

A cheese *burek* filled with parsley, garlic, black pepper, and cream tempts the hungry snacker.

mountain lakes, and rivers; and truffles and other less exotic mushrooms fresh from the wooded hills of Istria. Such abundance has left its mark on eating habits.

Regional specialties, still very much part of Croatian diets, include *visovačka begavica* (VEE-so-vahtch-kah BE-gah-vee-tsah), a savory lamb cooked in ewe's milk in the Šibenik area and turkey with *mlinci* (MLEEN-tsee), or small, flat dumplings, in Zagorje and Slavonia. In Dalmatia, *pašticada* (PASH-ti-tsada), a sweet-and-sour beef stew or pot roast, reigns supreme. In the Zagorje area, *zagorska zlevka* (ZAH-gor-skah ZEH-lev-kah), a corn flour cake, is well known. On Pag Island, the specialty is a pungent hard cheese served with olives, and *tartufi* (TAHR-too-fee), wild truffles on a pasta base, are special to the Istria area.

Snack food is cheap and common in all towns throughout the country. It is often of Turkish origin. Some examples are *cevapčići*, (CHE-vahp-chee-chee), or spicy beef or pork meatballs; *ražnjići* (RAHZH-nyee-chee), or kebab; and *burek* (BOO-rek), a pastry stuffed with either meat or cheese.

DESSERT

It is difficult to find a Croatian who does not have a sweet tooth, and an abundance of cakes satisfies this craving. Many people feel that dinner is incomplete without *orahnjača* (o-RAH-nyah-chah), a ground walnut roll made with a sweet yeast dough. *Kremsnita*, a custard cream cake, is a favorite dessert throughout Croatia and the surrounding European countries.

EATING OUT

Croatians love to eat with company. By far the most popular place to gather is the *gostionica* (gos-TEEO-nee-tsah) or *konoba* (KO-no-bah). Both terms mean "restaurant-pub." *Restauracija* (RES-tah-oo-rah-tsee-yah), or "restaurants proper," tend to be slightly more expensive and have lost out in the competition to provide quality food and drink in the quantities that Croatians demand in exchange for their hard-earned kuna.

Self-service cafeterias have caught on in towns, particularly Zagreb, and they offer good, cheap food but a less social atmosphere. They are popular in Croatia as convenient and quick places for lunch.

People eat at an outdoor café in the Old Town section of Dubrovnik.

INTERNET LINKS

https://www.croatia-expert.com/croatian-food
This site provides a good overview of Croatia's regional cuisines.

https://www.frankaboutcroatia.com/croatian-food
Regional specialties with descriptions and photos are listed on this travel site.

https://www.nytimes.com/2016/11/20/travel/croatia-truffles -istria-italy.html
This article describes truffle hunting in Croatia.

DALMATINSKA PAŠTICADA

This traditional Dalmatian beef pot roast is usually served with gnocchi or pasta.

3 to 4 pounds beef round, or other cut of stewing beef

6 whole cloves

2 cups red wine vinegar

½ cup cooking oil

5 cloves garlic, sliced

6 slices bacon, coarsely chopped

3 onions, 2 carrots, and 1 small celery root, peeled and chopped

2 Tbsp chopped fresh rosemary

1 Tbsp flour

2 Tbsp tomato paste

1 Tbsp sugar

2 cups beef broth

½ cup dry red wine

1 cup pitted prunes

1 Tbsp dijon mustard

salt and pepper

Place the beef in a large dish or plastic bag. Cover with vinegar and cloves. Cover, and leave overnight in the refrigerator. The next day, remove the meat from the vinegar. Remove cloves. Pat dry, and sprinkle generously with salt and pepper.

Add oil to a Dutch oven, and brown the meat on all sides over a medium-high heat. Remove meat, and set aside. Sauté the bacon and vegetables in the same oil until lightly browned. Sprinkle with flour, stir, and cook for one more minute. Add beef broth and stir.

Return the meat to the pot. Add the tomato paste, wine, and sugar. Bring to a boil, cover and turn down to a simmer. Cook covered on low heat for 2 hours; then add prunes and apples. Recover, and cook for another hour or until the meat is very tender. When the meat is tender, remove it to a plate, and cut into thick slices. Add mustard to the sauce in the pot. Purée the vegetables and sauce with a hand blender. Adjust seasoning.

Serve with gnocchi or noodles. Garnish with parsley or grated parmesan cheese.

KREMSNITA (CUSTARD CREAM CAKE)

2 puff pastry sheets (store bought; thawed
   according to directions on package)
4 cups whole milk
8 eggs, separated
1 cup sugar
1¼ cups flour
2 Tsp vanilla
3 cups heavy whipping cream
2 Tbsp powdered (confectioners') sugar, plus
   more for sprinkling

Preheat the oven to 350°F (175°C).

Pastry: On a lightly floured work surface, roll each sheet of puff pastry into a 9-inch x 13-inch rectangle. Place the pastry on a baking sheet and bake for ten minutes.

Remove the pastry from the oven, and set aside to cool completely.

Custard: In a large bowl, beat egg yolks with sugar until light and fluffy. Slowly add flour, vanilla extract, and 1 cup of milk until well combined. Set aside.

Over medium heat, boil remaining 3 cups of milk in a saucepan. Slowly stir in egg yolk mixture, and keep stirring until thickened. Remove from heat and set aside.

In a large bowl, beat the 8 egg whites until very stiff. Fold into the custard.

Assemble: Place one pastry sheet on the bottom of a 9-inch x 13-inch baking dish. Pour the custard over the pastry. Place plastic wrap over custard and chill in the refrigerator for a few hours until cooled and firm.

Beat the heavy whipping cream with the powdered sugar until firm peaks form. Pour over the chilled custard and smooth. Cut the second pastry sheet into 15 squares. Place over the custard cake in neat rows and sprinkle with more powdered sugar.

Serve cold by cutting between the pastry squares. Serves 15.

MAP OF CROATIA

Adriatic Sea, A3—A4, B4—B5

Bjelovar, C2
Bosnia and Herzegovina, B2—B3, C2—C4, D2—D5

Brač, C4

Cetina River, C4
Cres, A2—A3
Croatia-Slavonia, B2, C2

Dalmatia, B3
Danube River, D1—D2
Dinaric Alps, C4
Drava River, A1, B1, C1—C2, D2
Dubrovnik, D5
Dugi Otok, A3, B3—B4

Glina, B2
Gulf of Kotor, D5
Gulf of Venice, A2

Hungary, B1, C1—C2, D1—D2

Hvar, C4

Istria, A2
Istrian Peninsula, A2—A3
Italy, A1—A2, A4—A5

Karlovac, B2
Knin, B4
Korčula, C5
Kornat, B4
Krapina, B1
Krk, A2—A3
Krka River, B3—B4
Kupa River, B2

Lastovo, C5
Lošinj, A3

Makarska, C4
Medjugorje, C4
Medvednica Mountains, B2
Mljet, C5
Montenegro, D4—D5
Mount Dinara, B3

Neretva River, C4, D4

Osijek, D2

Pag, A3
Pannonian Plain, C2
Papuk Mountains, C2
Pašman, B4
Peljesac, C5
Plitvice Lakes, B3
Plješevica Mountains, B3
Ploče, C4
Poatija, A2
Porec, A2
Psunj Mountains, C2
Pula, A3

Rab, A3
Rijeka, A2
Roving, A2

Samobar, B2
Sava River, A1, B1—B2, C2—C3, D2—D3
Serbia, D2—D3
Šibenik, B4
Sinj, C4
Sisak, B2

Slovenia, A1—A2, B1—B2
Split, C4
Ston, C5

Trogir, B4

Uglian, B3

Varazdin, B1
Velebit Mountains, B3
Velika Kapela Mountains, B2—B3
Virovitica, C2
Vukovar, D2

Zadar, B3
Zagreb, B2

ECONOMIC CROATIA

Services

✈ Airports

🚢 Port

🧍 Tourism

Manufacturing

◆ Cement

🏭 Petroleum refineries

Natural Resources

🪙 Bauxite

⛽ Natural gas

🛢 Oil

ABOUT THE ECONOMY

All figures are 2017 estimates unless otherwise noted.

GROSS DOMESTIC PRODUCT (GDP, OFFICIAL EXCHANGE RATE)
$54.76 billion

GDP PER CAPITA
$24,700

LABOR FORCE
1.559 million

LABOR FORCE BY OCCUPATION
Agriculture: 1.9 percent
Industry: 27.3 percent
Services: 70.8 percent

CURRENCY
Kuna (HRK) *Note: Croatia is expected to adopt the euro in 2020.*
1 kuna = 100 lipa
US $1 = 6.65 HRK (April 2019)

UNEMPLOYMENT RATE
12.4 percent

POPULATION BELOW POVERTY LINE
19.5 percent

AGRICULTURAL PRODUCTS
arable crops (wheat, corn, barley, sugar beet, sunflower, rapeseed, alfalfa, clover); vegetables (potatoes, cabbage, onion, tomato, pepper); fruits (apples, plum, mandarins, olives), grapes for wine; livestock (cattle, cows, pigs); dairy products

INDUSTRIES
chemicals and plastics, machine tools, fabricated metal, electronics, pig iron and rolled steel products, aluminum, paper, wood products, construction materials, textiles, shipbuilding, petroleum and petroleum refining, food and beverages, tourism

EXPORTS
transportation equipment, machinery, textiles, chemicals, foodstuffs, fuels

EXPORT PARTNERS
Italy, Germany, Slovenia, Bosnia and Herzegovina, Austria, Serbia

IMPORTS
machinery; transportation and electrical equipment; chemicals, fuels, and lubricants; foodstuffs

IMPORT PARTNERS
Germany, Italy, Slovenia, Hungary, Austria

CULTURAL CROATIA

Pula

This three-thousand-year-old coastal town on the Istrian Peninsula is home to many examples of Roman architecture, including the Triumphal Arch of the Sergii, the Gate of Hercules, and the impressive Pula Arena amphitheater, which was constructed between 27 BCE and 68 CE.

Plitvice Lakes National Park

This popular tourist attraction includes sixteen beautiful lakes interconnected by a series of spectacular waterfalls. Granted UNESCO World Heritage status in 1979, the woodlands of the park teem with wildlife.

Diocletian's Palace

Located in the historic city of Split, Emperor Diocletian's palace is one of the most complete Roman architectural and cultural features on the Adriatic coast. Built in preparation for Diocletian's retirement in 305 CE, the complex includes religious buildings, the emperor's apartments, a mausoleum, and a basement. It is a UNESCO World Heritage site.

Cathedral of Saint James, Šibenik

Work began on the Cathedral of Saint James in 1402 and continued through to 1555. The structure is made entirely from stone and combines Gothic and Renaissance styles, including a frieze decorated with seventy-one sculptured faces of men, women, and children. The roof was damaged during the war but was quickly repaired. It has been on the UNESCO World Heritage List since 2000.

Old City (Old Town) of Dubrovnik

The historic district of the of Dubrovnik boasts old buildings, such as Renaissance-era Saint Sa Church and the Arbor Trsteno, the oldest arboretu the world, dating back to 1 The old city is surrounde a mile-long (1.6 km) turn wall that is 12–18 feet (5.5 meters) thick in places a UNESCO World Heritage

Trogir

Situated on the small island of Iovo, the historic city of Trogir has what is considered the best-preserved Romanesque-Gothic complex in all of Central Europe, made up of churches, towers, palaces, and walls from cultures as diverse as the ancient Greeks, Romans, and Venetians. In 1997, the town was added to the UNESCO World Heritage List of protected sites.

Historical Complex of Split

This UNESCO World Heritage site in the center of the old city of Split includes twelfth- and thirteenth-century churches, fifteenth-century palaces, medieval fortifications, and Diocletian's palace.

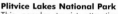

Stari Grad Plain

Situated on the island of Hvar, the Stari Grad Plain is the largest and most fertile plain in all the Adriatic islands. In the fourth century BCE, the plain was divided into seventy-five parcels in the shape of an elongated 2,952 by 590 feet (900 by 180 meters) rectangle, one of the earliest examples of land allocation in Europe. The Greek field layout is still intact, thanks to continuing maintenance of its dry stone walls. In 2008, the Stari Grad Plain was added to the UNESCO World Heritage List.

ABOUT THE CULTURE

All figures are 2018 estimates unless otherwise noted.

OFFICIAL NAME
Republika Hrvats (Republic of Croatia)

LAND AREA
21,611 square miles (55,974 sq km)

HIGHEST POINT
Mount Dinara (6006 feet/1,830 meters)

POPULATION
4,270,480

POPULATION GROWTH RATE
—0.51 percent

ETHNIC GROUPS
Croat 90.4 percent, Serb 4.4 percent, other 4.4 percent (including Bosniak, Hungarian, Slovene, Czech, and Romani), unspecified 0.8 percent (2011 estimate.)

RELIGION
Roman Catholic 86.3 percent, Orthodox 4.4 percent, Muslim 1.5 percent, other 1.5 percent, unspecified 2.5 percent, not religious or atheist 3.8 percent (2011 est.)

LANGUAGES
Croatian (official) 95.6 percent, Serbian 1.2 percent, other 3 percent (including Hungarian, Czech, Slovak, and Albanian), unspecified 0.2 percent (2011 est.)

LIFE EXPECTANCY
Total population: 76.3 years
Male: 73.2 years
Female: 79.6 years

FERTILITY RATE
1.42 children born per woman

INFANT MORTALITY RATE
9.1 deaths/100,000 live births (2015)

LITERACY RATE
99.3 percent (2015)

TIMELINE

IN CROATIA	IN THE WORLD
600	**600 CE**
Croats settle in the area between the Adriatic Sea and the Sava and Drava rivers.	Height of the Maya civilization is reached.
1526	
Croatia unites with Austria.	**1530**
	The African transatlantic slave trade begins.
	1776
	US Declaration of Independence is signed.
	1789–1799
1871	The French Revolution takes place.
The Rakovica Revolt against Austria-Hungary fails to establish an independent Croatian state.	
	1914
1918	World War I begins.
Croatia joins the Kingdom of Serbs, Croats, and Slovenes.	
1929	
The kingdom becomes Yugoslavia.	**1939**
1941	World War II begins.
Nazi Germany invades Yugoslavia. A fascist puppet government, the Ustaše, is installed.	
1945	**1945**
Croatia becomes a republic of the Yugoslav Socialist Federation.	The United States drops atomic bombs on Japan. World War II ends.
	1969
	US astronaut Neil Armstrong becomes first person on the moon.
	1986
1990	Nuclear power disaster occurs at Chernobyl.
First free elections in fifty years are held in Croatia. Franjo Tudjman wins.	
1991	**1991**
Croatia declares its independence from Yugoslavia. Civil war breaks out.	Breakup of the Soviet Union occurs.
1995	
Tudjman signs the Dayton Peace Accords.	
1996	
Croatia restores diplomatic relations with Yugoslavia. Croatia joins the Council of Europe.	

IN CROATIA	IN THE WORLD
1997	**1997**
Tudjman is reelected as president.	Britain returns Hong Kong to China.
2000	
Ivica Raćan becomes the new prime minister the year after Tudjman's death. Stjepan Mesić is elected the new president.	**2001**
2002	Al-Qaeda terrorists stage 9/11 attacks in New York, Pennsylvania, and Washington, DC.
Prime Minister Raćan resigns as infighting within the coalition paralyzes economic reform.	**2003**
2005	War in Iraq begins.
President Stjepan Mesić wins second term.	
2008	**2008**
Parliament approves Prime Minister Ivo Sanader's new HDZ-led coalition government.	US elects first African American president, Barack Obama.
2009	**2009**
Croatia officially joins NATO. Prime Minister Ivo Sanader resigns. Jadranka Kosor becomes prime minister.	Outbreak of H1N1 flu spreads around the world.
2010	
Ivo Josipović of the opposition Social Democrats wins the presidential election.	
2013	
Croatia joins the EU.	
2014	
A Croatian court sentences Ivo Sanader to nine years in jail for siphoning millions in state money in his second corruption conviction.	
2015	**2015–2016**
Moderate conservative Kolinda Grabar-Kitarović is elected Croatia's first female president.	ISIS launches terror attacks in Belgium and France.
2017	**2017**
Ethnic Serb former paramilitary commander Dragan Vasiljković is convicted of war crimes during the conflict in the early 1990s.	Donald Trump becomes US president. Hurricanes devastate Houston, Caribbean islands, and Puerto Rico.
	2018
	Winter Olympics are held in South Korea.
	2019
2020	Terrorist attacks mosques in New Zealand.
Croatia is scheduled to adopt the euro.	Notre Dame Cathedral in Paris damaged by fire.

GLOSSARY

alka (AHL-kah)
A Croatian game played in Sinj, which celebrates the 1715 defeat of the Turks.

breks (BREKS)
Truffle-hunting dogs.

brodet (BRO-det)
An Istriana-style fish stew.

burek (BOO-rek)
A rich pastry stuffed with meat or cheese.

dovidjenja (DO-vee-jen-yah)
A Croatian word for "good-bye."

Glagolitic script
An ancient Croatian writing thought to have been invented by a Greek missionary named Cyril.

gostionica (gos-TEEO-nee-tsah)
A family-run restaurant.

kino (KEE-no)
A low-priced and very popular cinema where Croatians watch mostly foreign films.

kolo (KO-lo)
A Slavic dance where people dance in a circle.

kulen (KOO-len)
A paprika-flavored sausage.

kuna
The Croatian currency prior to the euro.

orahnjača (o-RAH-nyah-chah)
Croatian yeast rolls made with sugar and ground walnuts.

palaćinka (PAH-lah-cheen-kah)
Pancakes filled with jam and topped with chocolate.

ražnjići (rahzh-NYEE-chee)
A kebab.

Sabor
The Croatian parliament.

tamburica
A traditional three- or five-string lute.

Ustaše (OOS-tah-she)
The World War II fascist regime in Croatia.

zdravo (ZDRAH-vo)
A Croatian word for "hello."

županijas (zhoo-PAH-nee-yahs)
Regional counties.

FOR FURTHER INFORMATION

BOOKS

Chomsky, Noam. *Yugoslavia: Peace, War, and Dissolution*. Oakland, CA: PM Press, 2018.

DK Travel. *DK Eyewitness Travel Guide Croatia,* New York, NY: DK Publishing, 2019.

Tanner, Marcus. *Croatia: A Nation Forged in War*. New Haven, CT: Yale University Press, 2010.

ONLINE

BBC News. Croatia Profile: Timeline. https://www.bbc.com/news/world-europe-17217954

CIA. *The World Factbook*. "Croatia." https://www.cia.gov/library/publications/the-world-factbook/geos/hr.html

Croatia.eu. http://croatia.eu/index.php?lang=2

Find-Croatia. https://www.find-croatia.com

Lonely Planet. "Croatia: History." https://www.lonelyplanet.com/croatia/history#345093

UNESCO World Heritage List. https://whc.unesco.org/en/statesparties/hr

MUSIC

Fa Zagreb-Markovac. *Croatian Folklore Gold*. CD Baby, 2018.

Ned Benvin. *Croatian Folk Party*. CD Baby, 2016.

Klapa Cambi. *Songs of Croatia: Klapa Singing from the Dalmatian Coast*. ARC Music, 2007.

Tamburica Orchestra Veritas. *Folklore from Croatia*. 2009

FILMS

Cities of the World: The Islands of Croatia. TravelVideoStore.com, 2009.

Rick Steves' Europe, Episodes 1—3. New Video, 2010.

Slovenia and Croatia. TravelVideoStore.com, 2007.

BIBLIOGRAPHY

BBC News. Croatia Profile: Timeline. https://www.bbc.com/news/world-europe-17217954.

Capps, Kriston. "'Game of Thrones' Tourists Are Besieging Dubrovnik." Citylab, December 11, 2017. https://www.citylab.com/design/2017/12/game-of-thrones-tourists-are-beseiging-dubrovnik/544967.

CIA. *The World Factbook*. "Croatia." https://www.cia.gov/library/publications/the-world-factbook/geos/hr.html.

Croatia.eu. http://croatia.eu/index.php?lang=2.

Croatian Forest Research Institute. "Forests and Forestry in Croatia," 2015. http://www.sumins.hr/wp-content/uploads/2016/11/Bro%C5%A1ura_FACESMAP_Forests-in-Croatia.pdf.

Encyclopaedia Britannica. "Croatia." https://www.britannica.com/place/Croatia.

Find-Croatia. https://www.find-croatia.com.

Global Information, Inc. "Construction in Croatia: Key Trends and Opportunities to 2022." September 28, 2018. https://www.giiresearch.com/report/time246477-construction-croatia-key-trends-opportunities-2015.html.

History on the Net. "World War One—Assassination of Franz Ferdinand." https://www.historyonthenet.com/world-war-one-assassination-of-franz-ferdinand.

Judah, Tim. "Yugoslavia: 1918—2003." BBC History. http://www.bbc.co.uk/history/worldwars/wwone/yugoslavia_01.shtml.

Lonely Planet. "Croatia: History." https://www.lonelyplanet.com/croatia/history#345093.

UNESCO Intangible Cultural Heritage of Humanity. https://ich.unesco.org/en/state/croatia-HR.

UNESCO World Heritage List. https://whc.unesco.org/en/statesparties/hr.

United Nations Economic Commission for Europe. Croatia: Environmental Performance Reviews. Second Review, 2014. http://www.unece.org/fileadmin/DAM/env/epr/epr_studies/ECE_CEP_172_En.pdf.

INDEX

Adriatic Sea, 5, 9, 11—12, 18, 26, 111, 125, 133, 138
agriculture, 16, 52—53, 64, 83, 135
alphabet, 95
animals, 17, 67—70, 115
Austria, 29—30, 75, 125, 135, 138
Austro-Hungarian, 30—31, 33, 76, 78, 103

Balkans, 5, 11, 24, 31, 37-38, 47, 50, 53, 55, 57, 61, 67, 71, 87, 107—108
beaches, 6, 8, 11—12, 111
birds, 17, 66, 68
Bosnia and Herzegovina, 11, 14, 26, 31, 34, 37, 47, 52, 55, 57, 60—61, 69, 75, 89—90, 93, 95, 133, 135
Brač, 12, 62, 107, 121, 133

Carnival, 8, 104, 118—120
cathedrals, 13, 86—87, 136, 139
Catholicism, 9, 26, 42, 87—90, 119, 136—137
Charlemagne (Charles the Great), 27
children, 61, 81—83, 85, 104, 114, 119, 123, 136—137
Christianity, 25—27, 76, 87—89, 95, 119
Christmas, 9, 41, 119, 121—123
cities, 19—21, 56, 83, 90, 112
coast/coastline, 5, 6, 7—8, 11—12, 15—17, 24, 28—29, 53, 59—60, 62, 66, 68—70, 79, 95, 108, 111, 116, 125
communism, 33—35, 43, 49, 55, 60, 76, 88, 94, 111
constitution, 41—42, 44—47, 74, 96
Croats, 5, 26—28, 31—32, 36—38, 75—78, 88, 90—91, 94, 100, 112, 121, 138
crops, 16, 135

Dalmatia, 8, 11, 13, 15, 19, 24—30, 51, 53, 66, 69, 78, 79, 94—95, 104, 108, 112, 125, 128, 130
Danube River, 20, 24, 57, 60, 62, 133
Dayton Peace Accords, 37, 139

diaspora, 75—76
Dinaric Alps, 12, 17, 133
Diocletian, 21, 25—26, 39, 121, 138
Drava River, 16, 18, 60, 133, 138
Dubrovnik, 6—8, 13, 15, 19—21, 28, 36, 54, 57, 64, 82—83, 90, 94—95, 97, 104, 111—112, 122—124, 129, 133

Eastern Orthodox Catholicism, 26, 74, 87, 89
education, 9, 47, 50, 75, 83, 85, 90, 114
endangered animals, 67—70
energy, 16, 19, 50, 55, 59
ethnic cleansing, 36, 38
euro, 55, 139
Europe, 5, 9, 11, 13, 16—17, 19, 21, 23—24, 26, 31, 35—37, 53, 55—57, 59, 61, 63, 66, 68, 74—76, 93, 96, 99, 106, 108, 111, 126, 136, 139
European Union (EU), 6, 9, 36—37, 39, 46—50, 54—55, 57, 59—60, 63, 66, 71, 79, 81, 85, 109, 117, 139

family, 42, 81—83, 85, 106, 108, 117, 121
farming, 16, 52—53, 83
fish, 17, 59, 66, 115, 125—126
folk art, 99, 107—108
folk costumes, 72, 79, 106—107
folk dance, 104, 110—111
folklore, 8, 75, 79, 88, 108, 127
folk music, 104, 108, 110—111
football, 113, 117
forests, 13, 16—17, 52—53, 59—60, 62—64, 84, 111, 115, 126—127
Franks, 9, 26—27
freedom, 87, 91, 96—97, 103
freedom of the press, 96—97

Game of Thrones, 7, 54
Germany, 34, 75, 99, 113, 135, 138
Grabar-Kitarović, Kolinda, 42, 44
Greek, 5, 15, 24—26, 95
gross domestic product (GDP), 50, 52—53, 83, 135

health, 81, 84—85, 116
Heraclius, 26
Hungary, 11, 16, 26, 28—31, 60, 75, 78, 96, 125—126, 133, 135, 137
Hvar, 12, 21, 70, 104, 106—107, 121, 133

Illyria, 112
Illyrian Movement, 30, 78
Illyrians, 24
independence, 5—6, 20, 35—36, 38, 43, 47, 49, 60—61, 73, 76, 83, 88—89, 94, 111, 117, 119, 122, 138—139
Intangible Cultural Heritage, 104, 109, 120, 123
International Court of Justice, 38
Islam, 87, 89
islands, 5—6, 11—12, 15, 21, 24, 46, 55, 57, 59, 61—62, 65—66, 68, 70, 94—95, 104, 106—107, 111, 115, 121—122, 128, 136, 139
Istria, 9, 11, 29, 56—57, 66, 77, 94, 102, 104, 122, 125, 127—128, 133, 136
Italy, 9, 11, 52, 66, 75, 100, 105, 117, 125, 127, 133, 135

Jews, 32, 74, 88, 90—91

Kingdom of Croatia, 30
Kingdom of Serbs, Croats, and Slovenes, 31—32, 138
Korčula, 11
Krapina, 22—23, 133
kremsnita, 128, recipe, 131
Krk, 11—12, 55, 57, 94—95, 133
Krleža, Miroslav, 103, 105
kuna, 55, 59, 129, 135

lacemaking, 106—107
land mines, 61, 71
languages, 26, 30—31, 47, 75, 78, 83, 88, 92—97, 99, 101, 103, 105, 107, 137

INDEX

Macedonia, 24, 34, 47
marriage, 41—42, 81
media, 96—97
Mediterranean Sea, 7, 11—12, 15, 23, 68, 70, 125
Medjugorje, 90, 133
Mesić, Stjepan, 139
Milošević, Slobodan, 38
Mljet, 12, 15, 21, 66, 133
Montenegro, 11, 34—35, 47, 133
mountains, 11—12, 14, 16—17, 19, 66—68, 114, 128, 133
museums, 22—24, 111
music, 99—100, 107—108, 111—112, 121—123
Muslims, 74, 76, 87, 89, 96, 137

Napoleon, 28—29
national holidays, 119, 122—123
national parks, 5, 10, 13—15, 17, 64—66, 68, 70
NATO, 34, 37, 39, 46—47, 53, 139
Natura 2000, 63, 71
Neretva, 16, 18, 60, 133

Odyssey, 15
Olympics, 113—114, 139
Ottomans, 28—29, 75, 89, 93, 101, 121

Pag, 12, 21, 59, 106—107, 128, 133
Pannonian region, 5, 12, 16—17, 27, 52, 79, 107, 133
parliament, 29, 31, 40—41, 44, 46, 60, 139
pašticada, 128, recipe, 130
Plenković, Andrej, 39, 44
Plitvice Lakes, 13—14, 66, 70, 133
pollution, 8, 60, 115
Pula, 21, 57, 83, 100, 112, 133, 136

Ragusa Republic, 28
rivers, 16, 18—20, 24, 57, 59—60, 62, 126, 128, 133, 138
Romans, 5, 9, 21, 24—27, 30, 73—74, 82, 84, 87—88, 112, 121, 129, 136—137

Roman Empire, 24—26
Romani (Roma) people, 74, 137
Rome, 26, 88
ruins, 5—6, 13, 21, 25, 121

Sabor, 29, 40, 44
same-sex marriage, 41—42
Sanader, Ivo, 37, 39, 139
Sava River, 16, 18—19, 57, 60, 62, 133, 138
schools, 83, 102, 107, 115, 122
Serbia, 7, 11, 20, 26, 31—32, 34—38, 50, 53, 55, 73, 94—96, 133, 135
Serbo-Croatian, 93
Serbs, 26, 28, 31—33, 35—38, 43—44, 73, 87—89, 91, 138—139
shipbuilding, 33, 50—51, 135
Slavic people, 26, 30, 93, 95
Slavonia, 8, 11, 29—30, 61, 78, 104, 125—126, 128
soccer, 113, 117
socialism, 9, 34—35, 138
Soviet Union, 33, 35, 139
Split, 13, 19, 21, 24—26, 39, 57, 83, 90, 98, 100, 106—107, 111—112, 121—123, 133, 138

tamburica, 108
Tito, 32—34, 79, 88, 105
Tomislav, 28, 83
tourism, 6—9, 12, 15, 20, 33, 53—54, 59, , 61—62, 64, 66, 77, 111—112, 115—116, 122—123, 135
truffles, 125, 127—128
Tudjman, Franjo, 35—37, 43, 79, 138—139
Turkey, 15, 25, 29, 70, 76, 108, 125, 128

UNESCO, 7, 13—14, 19, 21, 25, 36, 39, 54, 104, 106, 120, 123, 136
United Nations, 13, 36, 47, 102
United States, 17, 37, 44—47, 50—51, 53, 61, 75, 77, 81, 84, 91, 96, 113, 138
Ustaše, 32, 43, 88, 138

Venice, 7, 11—12, 29—30, 113, 133
Vukovar, 6, 20—21, 23, 36, 61, 133

war, 5—6, 20, 31—39, 43, 46—47, 49—51, 53, 61, 73, 76, 88—89, 91, 93—94, 103, 111, 117, 136, 138—139
War of Independence, 5—6, 20, 35—36, 47, 61, 73, 111
water, 6, 18, 59—60, 63, 84, 111, 113
weddings, 81—82
wolves, 17, 69, 71
women, 84—85, 96, 109, 136
World Heritage sites, 7, 13—14, 19—21, 25, 36, 39, 54, 104, 136
World War I, 31, 33, 76, 103, 138
World War II, 31—32, 36, 43, 76, 88—89, 91, 138

Yugoslavia, 5, 9, 31—36, 38—39, 41, 49, 75—76, 79, 84, 88, 90, 95—96, 103, 107, 114, 138—139
Yugoslavists, 31
Yugoslav Wars, 35, 38

Zadar, 19, 21, 57, 83, 106, 122, 133
Zagreb, 6, 8, 11, 15, 18—19, 29, 32—34, 36, 40, 42, 44—46, 52, 56—57, 63—64, 83, 86—88, 97, 100—103, 105—107, 112, 114, 116, 122—123, 125, 128—129, 133